EYES ON NATURE®

WEIRD CREATURES

Kidsbooks®

Table of Contents

Written by
Mary Kay Carson
Rebecca L. Grambo
John Grassy
and
Robert Matero

Scientific Consultants

Edward M. Spevak	David Dickey	Malcolm Fenton, Ph.D	Steven Bailey
Wildlife Conservation	Dept. of Herpetology	The Dalton School	Curator of Fishes
Society, Bronx Zoo	American Museum of		New England Aquarium
	Natural History		

WEIRD SEA CREATURES

Look closely! The weird-looking objects you see on these pages are not underwater plants or rocks. They are scorpion fish, which live mostly in the Pacific Ocean.

▲ DEADLY DISGUISES

For scorpion fish, being mistaken for the ocean bottom or part of a coral reef is a useful trick. The scorpion fish's natural camouflage lets it disappear into the background, where it holds still and waits. When other fish, not realizing the danger, swim close enough, wham! The scorpion fish opens its mouth, snaps up that fish, and gulps it down.

▲ ROCK OR FISH?

Look how close the scorpion fish resembles a coral reef! Can you spot the mouth and eye among the coral-reef camouflage on the scorpion fish?

Scorpionfish
(Scorpaena guttata) ▶

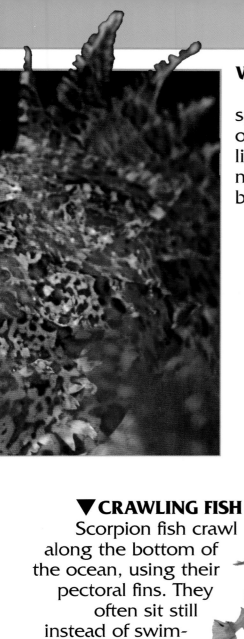

WATCH YOUR STEP! ▼

You don't want to step on a scorpion fish. Many have long spines, and some scorpion-fish spines are poisonous. When a diver or swimmer steps on a spine, it shoots poison into the foot just like a needle. This scorpionlike sting is where the fish gets its name. A scorpion fish's poison is strong enough to cause breathing problems and can kill a human.

▼CRAWLING FISH

Scorpion fish crawl along the bottom of the ocean, using their pectoral fins. They often sit still instead of swimming around to save it's energy.

The scorpion fish have a very appropriate nickname—"Rock Fish".

E-E-EELS

Eels look like underwater snakes. They aren't reptiles, though; they are fish. Most eels don't have scales. Their skin is covered in a protective layer of slippery mucus instead. There are many different kinds of eels, and many varieties of each kind.

HIDE-AND-SEEK ▼

Moray eels are hunters. They hide in the cracks and holes of coral reefs. When a fish or squid swims by, a moray will pop out and bite it.

Don't try petting a moray eel. It will give any bothersome visitor a nasty bite. Don't try biting back, either! Some morays are safe to eat, but the flesh of others can make humans sick—or even kill them.

WEIRD WOLF ▲

With its large head, big mouth, and long body, the wolf fish (or wolf eel) can look very weird. It has a lot of sharp teeth, and its bite can cause serious harm. Its strong jaws and teeth can bite off fingers, and can even chomp through steel and wood! Those powerful teeth are used to crush the wolf fish's favorite foods, such as starfish, crabs, and sea urchins.

Wolf fish live in cold, deep waters. Most live in the North Atlantic, from Maine to Iceland to the British Isles. Some live in the Pacific Ocean.

The wolf fish can grow to about 7 1/2 feet long and can weigh 20 pounds! You wouldn't want to meet one of these scary swimmers at feeding time!

FIRE MOUTHS ▶

The two dragon moray eels in this picture are not laughing or showing off their dental work. They have such long teeth that they can't close their mouths! The moray eel's wide mouth is filled with razor-sharp teeth, which help it grab its prey tightly.

It eats mostly fish, crustaceans (such as crabs), and other small marine animals.

◀ FRESH-WATER EELS

Freshwater eels are carnivores. They have large, pointed heads and slimy snake-like bodies. Freshwater eels are the most common type of eel for humans to eat!

TAKE A BITE! ▶

The moray eel's needle-shaped teeth can inflict serious wounds and cause severe bleeding and muscle damage to whatever—or whomever—it bites. The moray eel has been known to attack humans, but only when disturbed or provoked. Although it averages about 5 feet in length, some moray eels can grow almost 12 feet long. All eels are creepy, but the dragon moray has them all beat with its weird markings and deadly teeth!

PUFFERS AND PORKIES

Pufferfish and porcupinefish are part of a family of more than 100 species that have the ability to inflate their bodies with water or air. Blowfish, balloonfish, and bubblefish are only some of the many names these weird creatures are called. They "blow up" to scare or confuse predators.

▼**BEFORE**
All puffers are slow and clumsy swimmers, making them seem like easy prey.

▲**AFTER**
After a few quick gulps this puffer balloons up to three times its normal size. Take that, predator!

◄ PICK YOUR POISON

In addition to inflating and being covered with sharp spikes, many puffer species have yet another defense against predators. They can be very, very poisonous. Several parts of these fish (including the skin, muscles, and liver) are filled with an extremely strong poison. These toxins make them foul-tasting and sometimes lethal if an unlucky predator bites into one.

YIKES! SPIKES! ▼

Porcupinefish are armed from head to tail with prickly spikes. Although many are camouflaged in drab colors, others are dotted and brightly marked, warning predators that they can be toxic.

HUMANS, BEWARE! ▲

If eaten by humans, some of these fish can be deadly. In a few species, the poison in only one puffer can kill up to 30 humans! In spite of that, the flesh is a delicacy in some Asian countries, notably Japan. Specially trained chefs carefully remove the poisonous parts. But the chefs know that one mistake could lead to a fatal one.

TENTACLES, TENTACLES

An octopus can swim fast when it needs to. It jet-propels itself backward by shooting water out of its body. An octopus can also squirt an inky liquid at an enemy. The ink darkens the water, hiding the octopus and giving it time to swim to safety.

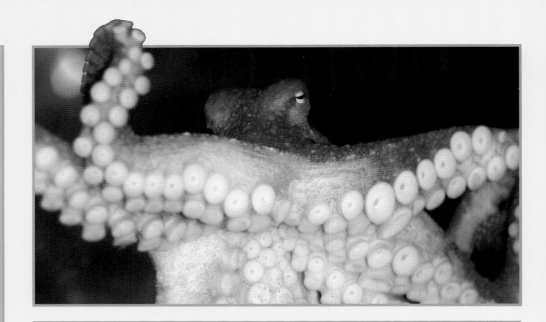

SQUID-TASTIC ▼
The head of a squid has eight arms, two tentacles and a horny beak for a mouth. The giant squid, which may grow to more than 40 feet long, has the biggest eyes of any living creature.

WORLD'S LARGEST ▲
This creature, the Pacific giant octopus, is the largest octopus in the world. This mollusk can weigh 100 pounds and measure 20 feet from arm tip to arm tip! (The world's smallest octopus is a lot smaller—only an inch across.) The Pacific giant octopus's main diet is crabs and lobsters, but it has been known to eat bigger fish—even sharks!

◄SUCTION CUPS

An octopus is all head, tentacles, and eyes. The underside of each of its eight tentacles is covered in suction cups. An octopus uses its sucker-covered tentacles to catch prey along the bottom of the sea. If an octopus loses an arm, it just grows a new one.

COLORS OF THE RAINBOW ▶

The octopus can turn many different colors. You can see the colors changing as you watch. The octopus has special, colored parts of its skin that it can make bigger or smaller within moments to hide itself on the seafloor.

IT'S A BLOB! ▼

The cuttlefish's soft body is not protected by a hard outer shell. Those "fingers" are actually its tentacles, which are attached to its large head.

Because it has no natural armor, this amazingly complex creature has a number of built-in defenses. It can change the color and texture of its skin to blend in with its surroundings. It can also squirt brown ink to cloud the water when danger is near. If threatened, the cuttlefish will bite, and that bite is poisonous.

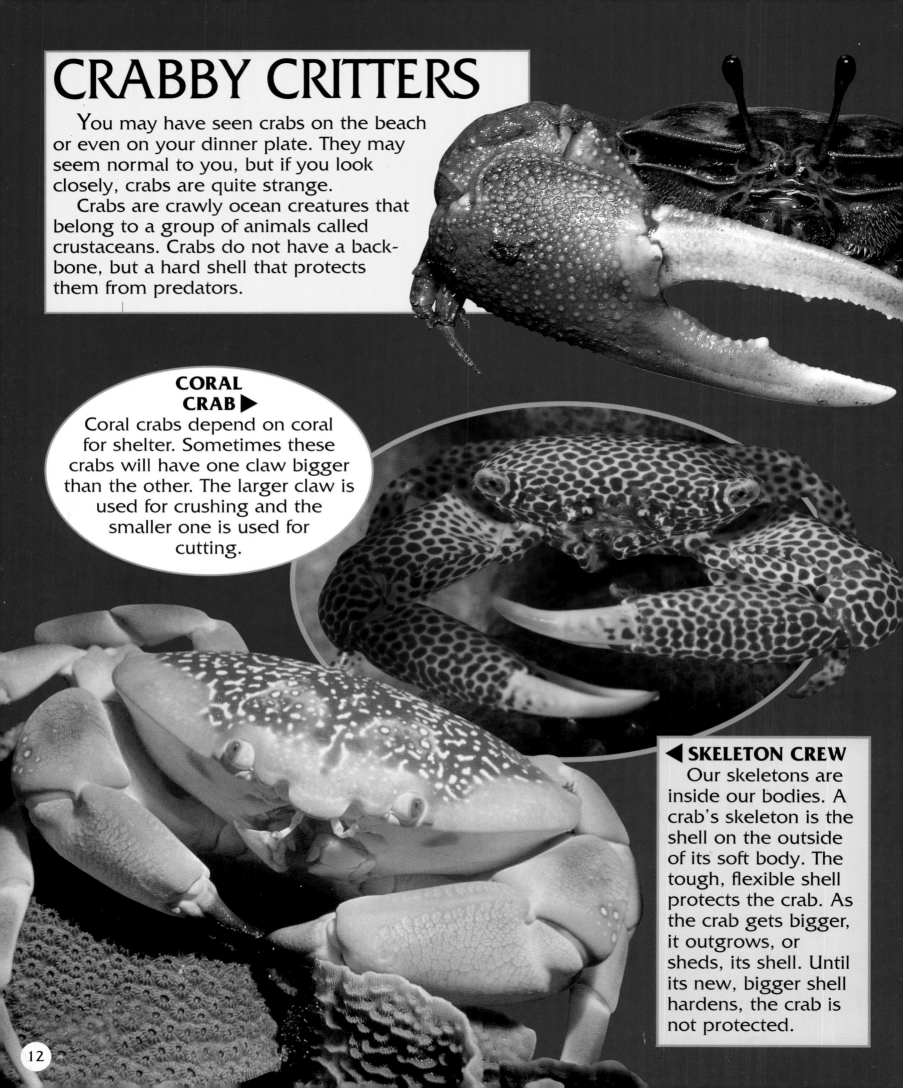

CRABBY CRITTERS

You may have seen crabs on the beach or even on your dinner plate. They may seem normal to you, but if you look closely, crabs are quite strange.

Crabs are crawly ocean creatures that belong to a group of animals called crustaceans. Crabs do not have a backbone, but a hard shell that protects them from predators.

CORAL CRAB ▶

Coral crabs depend on coral for shelter. Sometimes these crabs will have one claw bigger than the other. The larger claw is used for crushing and the smaller one is used for cutting.

◀ SKELETON CREW

Our skeletons are inside our bodies. A crab's skeleton is the shell on the outside of its soft body. The tough, flexible shell protects the crab. As the crab gets bigger, it outgrows, or sheds, its shell. Until its new, bigger shell hardens, the crab is not protected.

MATING CALL
Waving its oversized claw in the air, a male fiddler crab signals to females nearby. It also uses the big claw to defend its home. The really important job of gathering up food is done by the crab's small claw.

◀Hermit crabs live in second-hand seashells where they are protected from predators.

BUG EYES ▶
The eyes of a crab are beady and are on two stalks on top of their heads. The location of their eyes helps them see more of what is around them, so they can spot their prey more easily. Crabs also have two antennae, which have "smell detectors." These help crabs search for food.

CRAB WALK ▼
If you have seen a crab walk on the beach, you know why they are weird. Since their legs bend sideways, crabs walk or crawl from side to side instead of forward and backward. They have 10 legs, 2 of which are sharp pincers (PIN-shurs), or claws. The crab uses these claws to dig for, hold, and carry food; crack open shells of prey; and warn attackers. Crabs eat meat and plants; they are both predators and scavengers.

WEIRDOES OF THE DEEP

In 1872, the *Challenger* expedition of the British oceanographers proved beyond a doubt that there was life deep down in the ocean. Using scoops and dredges attached to ropes, they gathered samples of 4,417 new marine organisms! But scientists have only recently begun to fathom the mysteries of the deep.

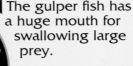

◀ The gulper fish has a huge mouth for swallowing large prey.

CLIFF HANGER

At a certain distance from each continent, the ocean floor drops sharply to a depth of 20,000 feet. In the very deep sea there is no sunlight, no plants, and the water is icy cold. Below a depth of 7,000 feet in any ocean, the temperature never rises above 39°F!

▼ This hatchetfish is being pursued by the viperfish (lower right), another deep-sea creature with light organs.

VOLCANIC CREATURES

Deep down on the ocean floor are vents that spew out scalding hot water. Warmed by liquid rock inside the earth, these springs are rich in minerals. Giant clams, tube worms twelve feet long, and blind crabs and shrimp the size of small dogs, all live near hot-water vents. They eat a special bacteria that manufactures its own food from the vent's gases and heat.

THE DARK SIDE ▲

You don't have to worry about running into one of these fierce-looking fish. Fangtooths make their home in the very deep, dark part of the ocean. They can survive in frigid black waters as deep as three miles below the surface.

It is hard to find a meal in this Dark Zone, where there is no light, no plants, and few animals. Fangtooths eat shrimps, small fish, or anything else that happens by.

Giant tube worms

DO NOT DISTURB ▶

In 1938, fishermen in the Indian Ocean netted a coelacanth, a fish believed to have been extinct for 100 million years! Scientists speculated that it had been living undisturbed in the deep sea.

UNDER PRESSURE

Animals living in the deep ocean have adapted to the tremendous pressure of the water. Most are so perfectly adapted to this environment that they cannot survive for long when brought up to the surface—the change in pressure is just too much.

BON APPETIT ▼

Did you ever wonder who keeps the ocean floor clean? Sea cucumbers help by eating the muddy surface and digesting what little food it contains.

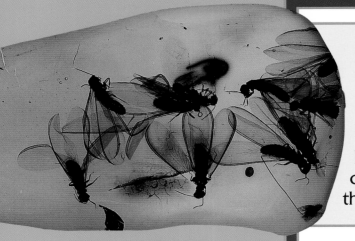

BUGS! BUGS! BUGS!

We live in a world of insects. Close to one million different species have been identified, making them the most abundant group of creatures on earth. From flies and bees to butterflies, ants, and beetles, insects are found all over the world. One acre of ground may be home to more than a million insects!

ANCIENT INSECTS ▲

Insects have been on Earth for more than 300 million years—since before the days of the dinosaurs! We have found insect fossils (like these termites, trapped in amber) from long ago. Insects were the first creatures to develop wings and fly, which helped them escape from predators and find new places to live.

▼ This insect's name is the banded sphinx moth, or *Eumorpha fasciata*.

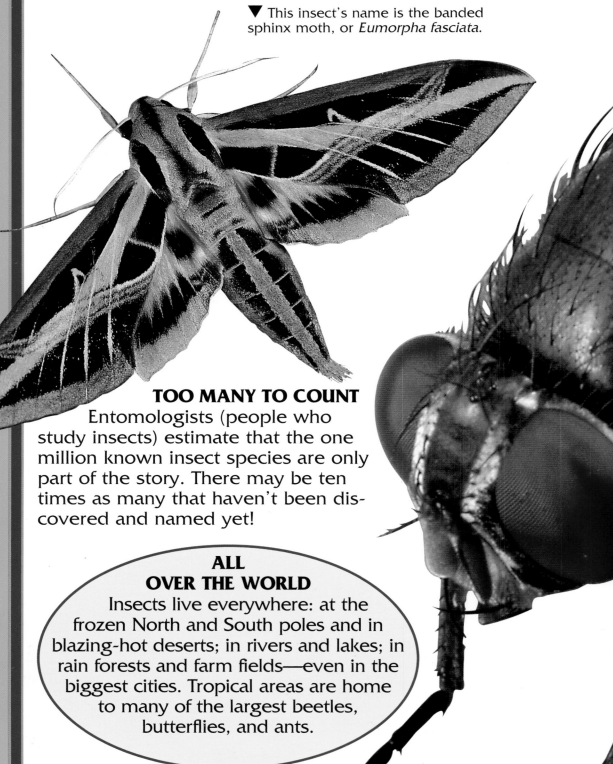

TOO MANY TO COUNT

Entomologists (people who study insects) estimate that the one million known insect species are only part of the story. There may be ten times as many that haven't been discovered and named yet!

SHAPES AND SIZES ▲

Some insects are so tiny that you need a magnifying glass or microscope to get a good look at them. Unmagnified, the flea above is just 1/16 of an inch long. Other insects are huge: The African giant swallowtail butterfly is as big as a bird, with a wingspan of six to ten inches.

ALL OVER THE WORLD

Insects live everywhere: at the frozen North and South poles and in blazing-hot deserts; in rivers and lakes; in rain forests and farm fields—even in the biggest cities. Tropical areas are home to many of the largest beetles, butterflies, and ants.

▼ Nobody likes flies, which is probably why we say "Buzz off!" to someone who is *bugging* us!

INSECTS AND PEOPLE

People have been fascinated by insects for a long time. Some we don't like—and some we do! In Japan and China, the symbol for *ant* comes from two other symbols: one that means *insect*, and one that means *unselfishness, justice,* and *courtesy*.

◀ HEY, I'M FLEXIBLE ▶

Insects are experts at finding the right places to live, hide, and eat. Leaf-cutter ants (right) eat fungus that they cultivate on leaves in warm, moist places. They thrive in tropical rain forests. Carpenter ants prefer dry, soft wood, so they are much happier in older, drier forests—or the walls of your house.

▲ AMAZING COLORS

Some of the coolest colors on any living thing belong to beetles. Just look at this rainbow wood-borer! In the Amazon rain forest and elsewhere, people use the colorful outer wing cases of jewel beetles to make necklaces and other jewelry.

INSECTS IN THE WEB OF LIFE

Only one percent of all insects are the pesky kind that cause problems. What do all the others do? In nature, all living things are part of the food chain. Insects are a major source of food for millions of different animal species. They do other important work, too.

▲ POLLINATORS

Lots of plants reproduce by making flowers—but the flowers can't make seeds until they get pollinated. Bees, butterflies, moths, and some beetles are pollinators: When they visit a flower to eat, they get covered with pollen, a soft powdery substance. They spread it as they go from flower to flower.

▲ RECYCLERS

Carrion beetles feed on yucky stuff, such as dead animals, fur, and feathers. They help prevent the spread of disease by turning waste materials into fresh new soil that is rich in nutrients. This helps plants grow, making food for other animals.

FISH FOOD

Water bugs, caddis flies, mayflies, and other insects live in or around water. They make great meals for all kinds of fish, as well as for frogs, salamanders, snakes, and other animals that live in or close to streams and lakes.

Giant water bugs carrying their eggs on their back.

BIRD FOOD ▶

Insects are food for many of the world's birds. Some swallows and warblers live on nothing but insects. It takes a lot of flies, gnats, and caterpillars to feed a nest of hungry babies, but there are always plenty of insects to go around! One third of all bird species would die off if there were no insects to eat.

▼ BUG EAT BUG

Insects are an important source of food for many animals, including other insects! Ladybugs feed on aphids; hornets and wasps eat caterpillars; ants eat the larvae of beetles and termites; and dragonflies zoom around catching gnats and mosquitoes.

BEAR FOOD

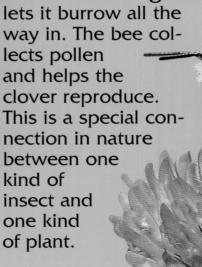

Can you believe that a 500-pound grizzly bear would eat moths? Every summer in some areas of the Rocky Mountains, grizzlies feast on hordes of army cutworm moths, scooping them up in big bunches with their paws. The moths are around for only a few weeks, so the bears gobble up all they can!

▼ YOU AND ONLY YOU

The flower on red clover is so big that most pollinators can't reach its nectar. But a bumblebee has the right stuff. Its massive body lets it burrow all the way in. The bee collects pollen and helps the clover reproduce. This is a special connection in nature between one kind of insect and one kind of plant.

INSECT EQUIPMENT

What makes an insect an insect? How can you distinguish insects from other creepy crawlies? It's not so hard. All of the world's insects have a few things in common.

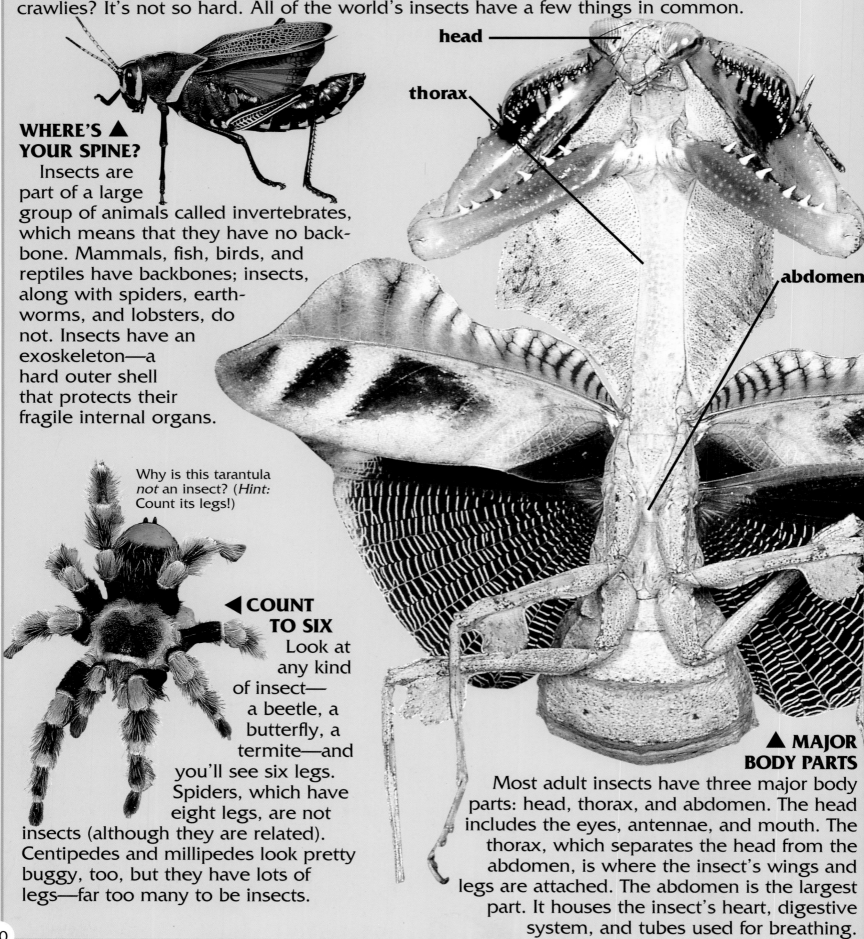

head

thorax

abdomen

WHERE'S ▲ YOUR SPINE?

Insects are part of a large group of animals called invertebrates, which means that they have no backbone. Mammals, fish, birds, and reptiles have backbones; insects, along with spiders, earthworms, and lobsters, do not. Insects have an exoskeleton—a hard outer shell that protects their fragile internal organs.

Why is this tarantula *not* an insect? (*Hint:* Count its legs!)

◄ COUNT TO SIX

Look at any kind of insect— a beetle, a butterfly, a termite—and you'll see six legs. Spiders, which have eight legs, are not insects (although they are related). Centipedes and millipedes look pretty buggy, too, but they have lots of legs—far too many to be insects.

▲ MAJOR BODY PARTS

Most adult insects have three major body parts: head, thorax, and abdomen. The head includes the eyes, antennae, and mouth. The thorax, which separates the head from the abdomen, is where the insect's wings and legs are attached. The abdomen is the largest part. It houses the insect's heart, digestive system, and tubes used for breathing.

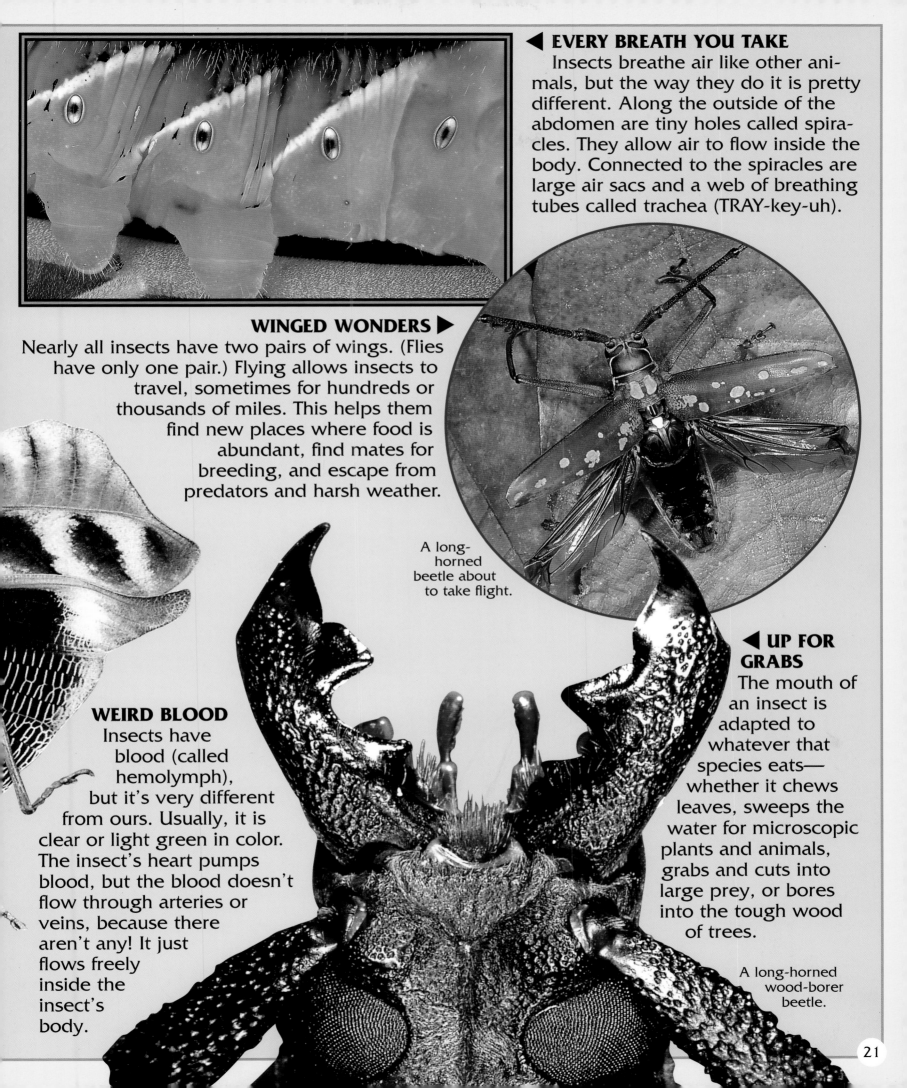

◄ EVERY BREATH YOU TAKE

Insects breathe air like other animals, but the way they do it is pretty different. Along the outside of the abdomen are tiny holes called spiracles. They allow air to flow inside the body. Connected to the spiracles are large air sacs and a web of breathing tubes called trachea (TRAY-key-uh).

WINGED WONDERS ►

Nearly all insects have two pairs of wings. (Flies have only one pair.) Flying allows insects to travel, sometimes for hundreds or thousands of miles. This helps them find new places where food is abundant, find mates for breeding, and escape from predators and harsh weather.

A long-horned beetle about to take flight.

WEIRD BLOOD

Insects have blood (called hemolymph), but it's very different from ours. Usually, it is clear or light green in color. The insect's heart pumps blood, but the blood doesn't flow through arteries or veins, because there aren't any! It just flows freely inside the insect's body.

◄ UP FOR GRABS

The mouth of an insect is adapted to whatever that species eats— whether it chews leaves, sweeps the water for microscopic plants and animals, grabs and cuts into large prey, or bores into the tough wood of trees.

A long-horned wood-borer beetle.

21

A BUG'S LIFE

A baby insect doesn't look much like it will as an adult. It goes through a number of big changes in its lifetime. This process of transformation is called *metamorphosis*, a word that means *a great change in body or appearance*.

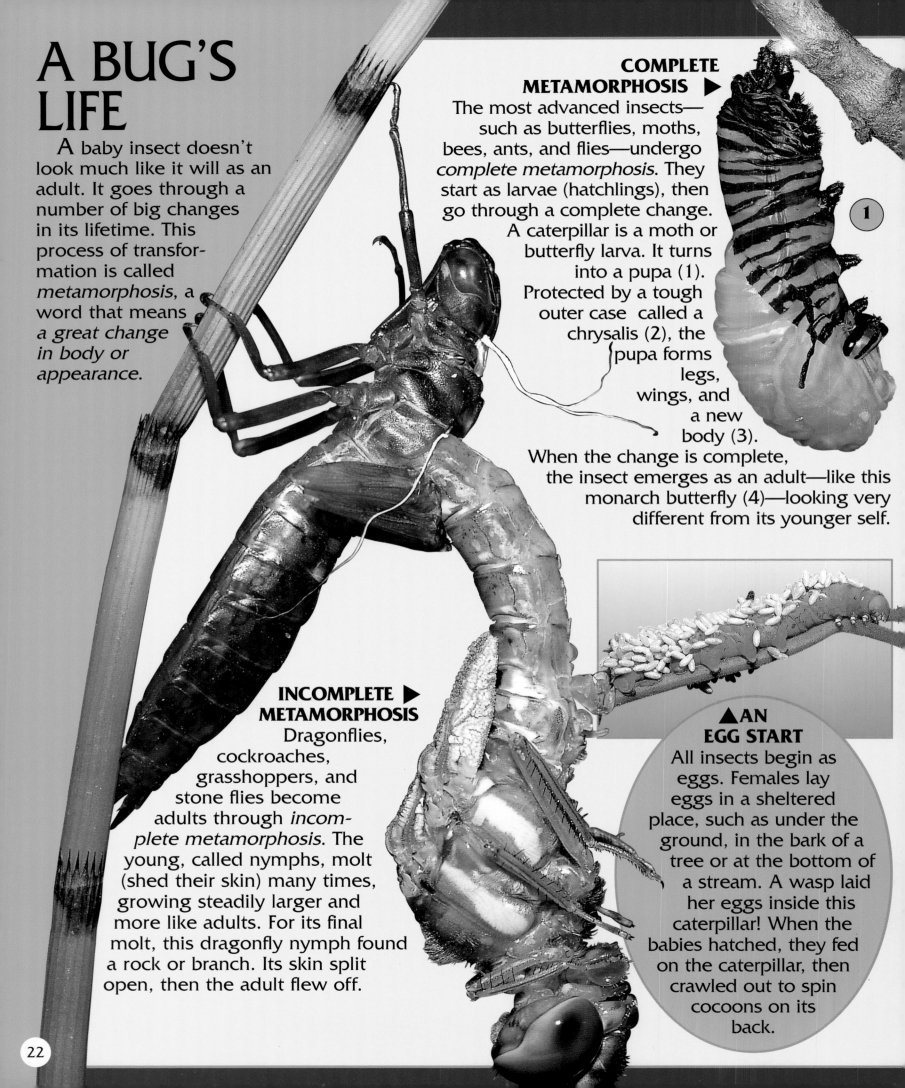

COMPLETE METAMORPHOSIS ▶

The most advanced insects—such as butterflies, moths, bees, ants, and flies—undergo *complete metamorphosis*. They start as larvae (hatchlings), then go through a complete change. A caterpillar is a moth or butterfly larva. It turns into a pupa (1). Protected by a tough outer case called a chrysalis (2), the pupa forms legs, wings, and a new body (3). When the change is complete, the insect emerges as an adult—like this monarch butterfly (4)—looking very different from its younger self.

INCOMPLETE ▶ METAMORPHOSIS

Dragonflies, cockroaches, grasshoppers, and stone flies become adults through *incomplete metamorphosis*. The young, called nymphs, molt (shed their skin) many times, growing steadily larger and more like adults. For its final molt, this dragonfly nymph found a rock or branch. Its skin split open, then the adult flew off.

▲ AN EGG START

All insects begin as eggs. Females lay eggs in a sheltered place, such as under the ground, in the bark of a tree or at the bottom of a stream. A wasp laid her eggs inside this caterpillar! When the babies hatched, they fed on the caterpillar, then crawled out to spin cocoons on its back.

1. New pupa
2. Chrysalis (KRIS-uh-lus)
3. Pupa nearing molt
4. Adult emerging

Praying mantis hatch-lings

◀ WHERE ARE MOM AND DAD?

Most insects grow up without parents around— they hatch and are soon on their way! But termites, ants, some wasps, and honeybees build large nests with special rooms for laying eggs, and spend a lot of time caring for their young. Some beetles also care for their eggs and newly hatched babies.

BUTTERFLIES AND MOTHS

With their awesome colors, shapes and sizes, butterflies and moths are some of the neatest insects around. You know that it's summer when you see them floating over flower gardens, ponds, and fields.

Sheep moth

▲ MOTH OR BUTTERFLY? ▼

How can you tell a moth from a butterfly? Moth antennae are lined with feathery hairs and have no club at the end; butterfly antennae have a small knob at the end. Moths rest with their wings out flat or angled like a tent; when butterflies rest, they fold their wings straight up.

California sisters butterfly

WILD BEAUTIES ▲

There are more than 170,000 kinds of butterflies and moths. They live just about everywhere, from high mountain meadows and cold, windy tundra to tropical rain forests, deserts, and woodlands. These monarch butterflies travel thousands of miles a year: They spend the summer in central and eastern North America, then fly to Mexico for the winter.

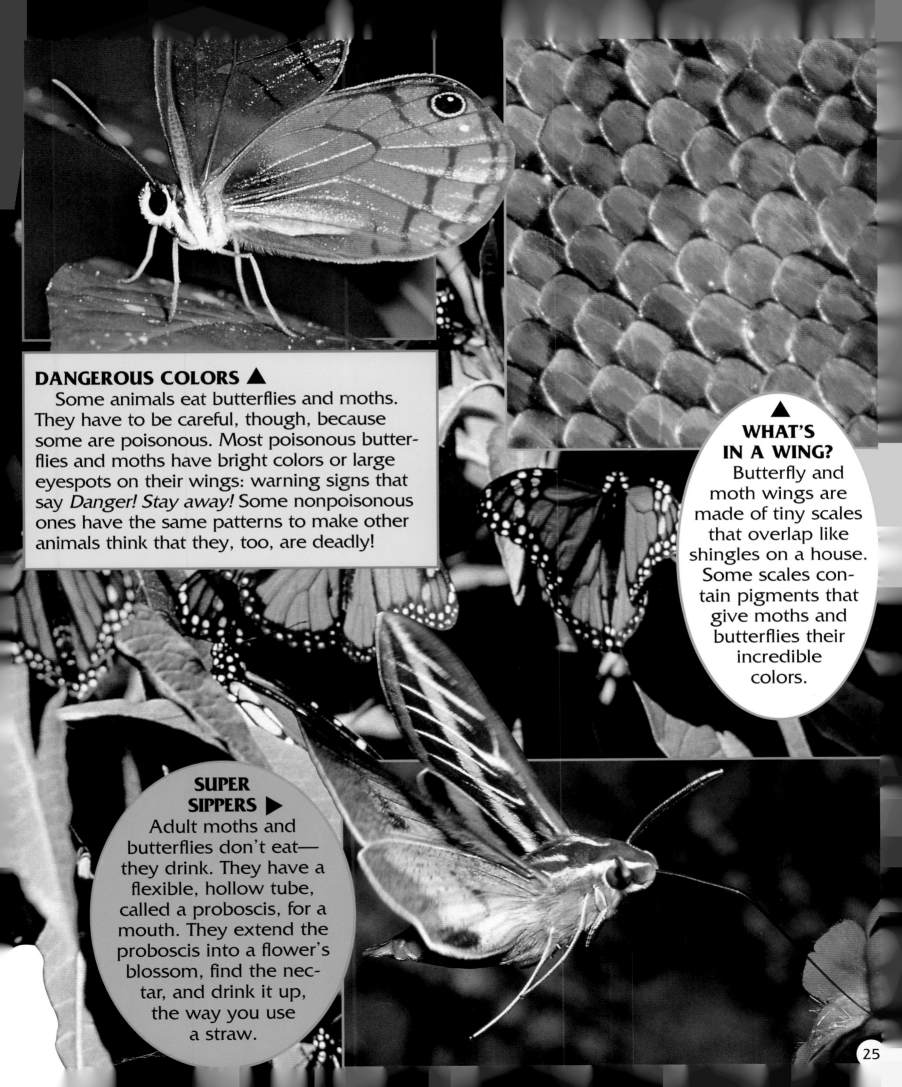

DANGEROUS COLORS ▲

Some animals eat butterflies and moths. They have to be careful, though, because some are poisonous. Most poisonous butterflies and moths have bright colors or large eyespots on their wings: warning signs that say *Danger! Stay away!* Some nonpoisonous ones have the same patterns to make other animals think that they, too, are deadly!

▲ WHAT'S IN A WING?

Butterfly and moth wings are made of tiny scales that overlap like shingles on a house. Some scales contain pigments that give moths and butterflies their incredible colors.

SUPER SIPPERS ▶

Adult moths and butterflies don't eat— they drink. They have a flexible, hollow tube, called a proboscis, for a mouth. They extend the proboscis into a flower's blossom, find the nectar, and drink it up, the way you use a straw.

HUNTERS AND HUNTED

Every single day, an insect must find enough food while making sure that other animals don't feed on it! But insects have been playing this game for millions of years, and have developed a lot of tricks to help them survive.

WHO GOES THERE?

Many mild-mannered insects have colors and shapes that make them look danger-ous—a trick called mimicry. This deadly-looking "snake" is really a cleverly disguised caterpillar.

▲ SPEED DEMON

The dragonfly is the fastest flier and has the keenest vision of any insect. It can see in almost every direction at once, and keeps its huge eyes clean by using special brushes on its front legs. Zooming after mayflies, mosquitoes, and other small insects, a dragonfly can hit 60 miles per hour! Male dragon-flies establish territories and will dive-bomb other males that get too close.

▲ ON THE PROWL

The front legs of the praying mantis, or mantid, are serrated for extra gripping power, to hold prey caught in its lightning-fast strike. Its head swivels in every direction, giving it excellent vision. Green or brown mantids blend with their surroundings, but the extra-tricky orchid mantid looks like a flower, drawing other bugs to its clutches.

BARK? TWIG? BUG? ▶

When this northern walkingstick stops moving, it looks like a twig, blending with its surroundings. Moths and butterflies have wing colors that match the leaves or bark of trees—even the shapes of some leaves! When they sit still, birds, rodents, and other predators can't see them!

If a young walkingstick loses a leg, it grows a new one when it molts!

◀ ROW, ROW, ROW

Water striders stay afloat on long legs coated with waxy, waterproof hairs, and use their middle legs like oars to move across water. They live on ponds, rivers, or oceans, eating insects that they find on the water's surface. (They eat each other, too!) They inject their prey with an enzyme that turns its head into mush.

◀ GET OUT OF THE WAY!

When a colony of driver ants swarms through the African forest on a hunting trip, even monkeys and snakes get out of their way! The worker ants kill and devour caterpillars, scorpions, cockroaches, as well as other ants. They are the most ferocious insects in the world, even attacking much larger prey!

This katydid's bigger-than-usual face helps scare away predators.

SEEING, HEARING, SMELLING

Nearly all insects have eyes and ears. Though seeing and hearing are useful, taste and smell are an insect's most important senses. Insects taste and smell the air, ground, and leaves and flowers of plants in order to determine what is and is not safe to eat.

ON YOUR TRAIL ▼

When most ants leave the colony to search for food, they leave a scent trail. The ant touches its abdomen to the ground, releasing a chemical that other ants read with their antennae. Usually, the trail leads to a new source of food—or back home.

▲ A BUG'S-EYE VIEW

Most insects have two large compound eyes, plus three smaller, simple eyes on top of their head. The compound eyes contain hundreds of individual eyes, called facets. Each facet gives the insect a separate picture of the world. You can see the many facets in this fly's eyes (magnified even more in the background photo).

◀ I HEAR YOU CALLING

Hearing is all-important for katydids. There are more than 100 types of katydids in North America and each has its own song, made by rubbing its wings together. Usually, only the males sing. They sing when it's time to mate, to help females find them.

GET THE PICTURE? ▼

The range of colors that many insects see is much different from what humans see. Insects can see ultraviolet, a color that is invisible to us. This may help a bee find the right flowers to feed on, or enable a bluebottle fly to find a mate.

▲ GOOD VIBRATIONS

The cricket has an ear on each front knee! Cricket ears work much like ours: An eardrum picks up vibrations in the air. Other insects have tiny hairs around the eyes and along the body that are sensitive to air movements and other changes in their surroundings.

SHOW ME THE WAY

Fireflies are beetles, not flies. On late summer evenings, firefly males and females put on a show as they locate one another for mating. The male goes first: He sends out a pattern of flashes as he flies, then waits for a female to reply. The light is produced by special cells in the firefly's abdomen.

SNIFFING AROUND

Insects with sharp eyes, such as wasps and dragonflies, have short antennae. Others, such as some beetles and moths (like this luna moth), have long antennae covered with tiny hairs. The antennae pick up smells in the air—from as far as 10 or 12 miles away! That makes smelling as good as seeing: They can find food, safety, and mates by smelling them!

29

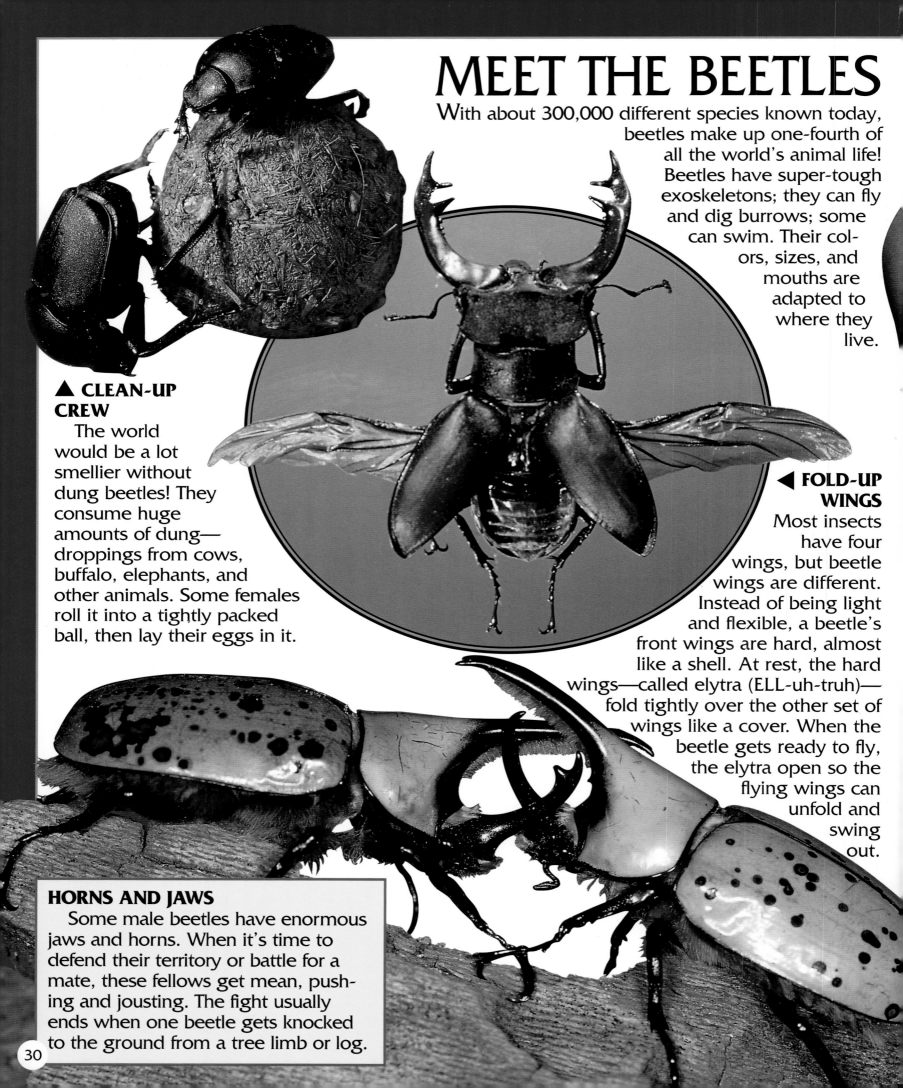

MEET THE BEETLES

With about 300,000 different species known today, beetles make up one-fourth of all the world's animal life! Beetles have super-tough exoskeletons; they can fly and dig burrows; some can swim. Their colors, sizes, and mouths are adapted to where they live.

▲ CLEAN-UP CREW

The world would be a lot smellier without dung beetles! They consume huge amounts of dung—droppings from cows, buffalo, elephants, and other animals. Some females roll it into a tightly packed ball, then lay their eggs in it.

◄ FOLD-UP WINGS

Most insects have four wings, but beetle wings are different. Instead of being light and flexible, a beetle's front wings are hard, almost like a shell. At rest, the hard wings—called elytra (ELL-uh-truh)—fold tightly over the other set of wings like a cover. When the beetle gets ready to fly, the elytra open so the flying wings can unfold and swing out.

HORNS AND JAWS

Some male beetles have enormous jaws and horns. When it's time to defend their territory or battle for a mate, these fellows get mean, pushing and jousting. The fight usually ends when one beetle gets knocked to the ground from a tree limb or log.

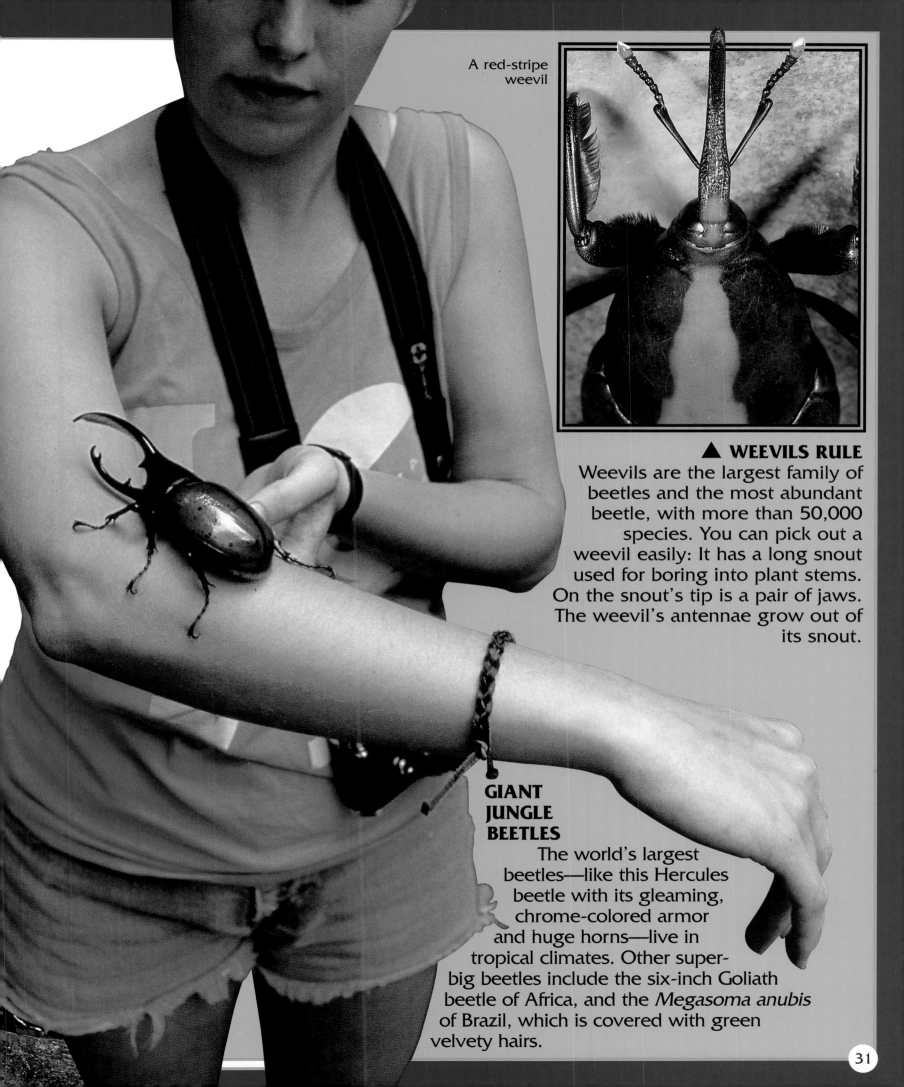

A red-stripe weevil

▲ WEEVILS RULE

Weevils are the largest family of beetles and the most abundant beetle, with more than 50,000 species. You can pick out a weevil easily: It has a long snout used for boring into plant stems. On the snout's tip is a pair of jaws. The weevil's antennae grow out of its snout.

GIANT JUNGLE BEETLES

The world's largest beetles—like this Hercules beetle with its gleaming, chrome-colored armor and huge horns—live in tropical climates. Other super-big beetles include the six-inch Goliath beetle of Africa, and the *Megasoma anubis* of Brazil, which is covered with green velvety hairs.

SOCIAL INSECTS

Most insects live on their own, coming together only when it's time to mate. But ants, honeybees, some wasps and hornets, and termites are social insects. They build large colonies, and each member has a job to do.

PAPIER-MÂCHÉ

A single paper-wasp queen starts a new colony each year. She chews up softened wood to make a soft, papier-mâché-like material for the nest. She lays eggs and raises the first worker wasps on her own. Then the workers, all females, take over. On hot days, they cool the nest by fanning their wings, or collecting water to spread over eggs and larvae.

SHAKE IT! ▶

Social insects need to know many things, such as where food is and whether danger is near. Honeybees perform a "dance" to let other worker bees know where nectar is. The dance provides important information—such as the direction, distance, and quantity of the nectar source.

DEFENDING THE COLONY ▶
For insects, protecting eggs and larvae from danger is job #1. If a predator threatens, worker ants scoop up their offspring and race off while soldier ants attack with biting jaws. Some soldier termites squirt a sticky goo at their enemies. Wasps and hornets swarm and sting when they smell an attack hormone released by other workers. *Yeeoww!*

▲ ALL HAIL THE QUEEN
All social insect colonies have a queen. Usually, she is larger than other members of the colony, and the only one able to lay eggs. The termite queen's abdomen becomes so swollen with eggs that she can hardly move!

HIGH-RISE HOMES
Compass termites live in Australia. They build huge, wedge-shaped mounds using soil and their own sticky secretions. Some of these towers stand 15 feet or higher and are just about waterproof. The narrow ends at the top of each mound always face north and south. If you're lost in the Australian outback, find one of these mounds and use it like a compass!

GOOD AND BAD INSECTS

There are many kinds of helpful insects. Bees produce honey and wax, silkmoth caterpillars make silk for clothing, and—for some people—insects make a nutritious, good-tasting meal! There are bad-guy bugs, too: a few kinds that make plenty of trouble for humans. It's never easy to stop them, but we keep trying!

TIMBER!

Many kinds of insects—including grasshoppers (pictured), beetles, and moths—eat the bark, leaves, and wood of trees. The larvae of spruce and pine beetles (called grubs) bore into the trunk of a living tree, weakening or killing it. Grasshoppers are defoliators, which means that they eat a tree's leaves, not the bark or wood.

STRANGE FRUIT ▲

The tiny fruit fly is one of the biggest pests in the world. Females lay eggs beneath the skin of fruits and vegetables. The larvae, called maggots, hatch soon after. The Mexican fruit fly attacks 50 different kinds of fruits and vegetables; the Mediterranean fruit fly attacks more than 250!

GOT SILK? ▶

Ever wonder why silk costs so much? It comes from specially bred and fed silkworms. Each silkworm cocoon is made of a single thread about 1,000 yards long. That thread must be carefully unwound and processed.

AS BUSY AS CAN BEE

From morning until dusk in summer, honeybees visit flowers. A single bee makes as many as 24 trips a day, and must stop at 100 to 1,500 flowers to fill itself with nectar. A fully loaded bee carries enough nectar to make one drop from an eyedropper. With enough bees, it all adds up: Two hives can make 150 pounds of honey in a year.

BUZZZZ ▲

There are more than 2,500 kinds of mosquitoes. Male mosquitoes eat nectar; only females drink blood. Besides spoiling outdoor fun, their bite can spread such fatal diseases as malaria and yellow fever to humans.

MAY I HELP YOU? ▶

Praying mantises help us out by doing what comes naturally—eating other bugs. The ones they like to eat are usually the same kinds that wreck crops and gardens. (They also enjoy a tasty lizard or frog now and then!)

INSECTS GET AROUND!

Insects are always looking for new places to live. They get into clothes and food shipments, airplanes and boats, luggage and boxes. Wherever people go, insects go, too. There is no way to stop them.

◀ PEST FROM OUT WEST

Long ago, the Colorado potato beetle ate only wild plants. But when American settlers moved west and began farming, it switched to the leaves of potato and tomato crops. No bug-killing chemical has stopped it yet. The beetle has taken hold across Europe and Asia, and recently showed up in China and Iran.

COTTON MENACE ▼

The boll weevil entered Texas (from Mexico) in 1892 and expanded its range by 60 miles each year. By 1922, it was destroying cotton fields throughout Alabama, Georgia, and other southeastern states. But it's a hero in Enterprise, Alabama: A statue honors it for forcing farmers there to switch to crops that turned out to be more profitable.

▲ FROM CANADA

European skipper butter-flies came to the U.S. from Canada about 80 years ago. You can now find their plump, furry bodies and brown-orange wings throughout New England. Another new population is grow-ing out west in Colorado and British Columbia. Butterfly experts believe that they may have hitched a ride on a shipment of hay.

NO KILLERS ▼

"Killer bees" are really African honeybees. Beekeepers took them to Brazil—then they escaped, breeding with other bees as they moved north. African bees are quick to defend their hives, but rarely attack people. Africanized bees make great honey. If you have a jar of honey at home, there's a good chance it was made by them.

THE CITY PEST ▼

Cockroaches, also called palmetto bugs, have been around for 280 million years. They are so tough that one can live for nearly three days *without its head*! Cockroaches live by the millions in urban areas, feeding on food scraps and other debris. They are *very* fast and can squeeze into the smallest spaces.

THEY'RE EVERYWHERE!

The cabbage butterfly is now so plentiful in the U.S. that it's hard to believe it's a relative newcomer. A native of England, it somehow got to Canada, where it took wing and spread throughout North America. The caterpillars feed on sour-tasting stuff—cabbage, peppergrass, and wild mustard—so it's no wonder birds don't like to eat them!

37

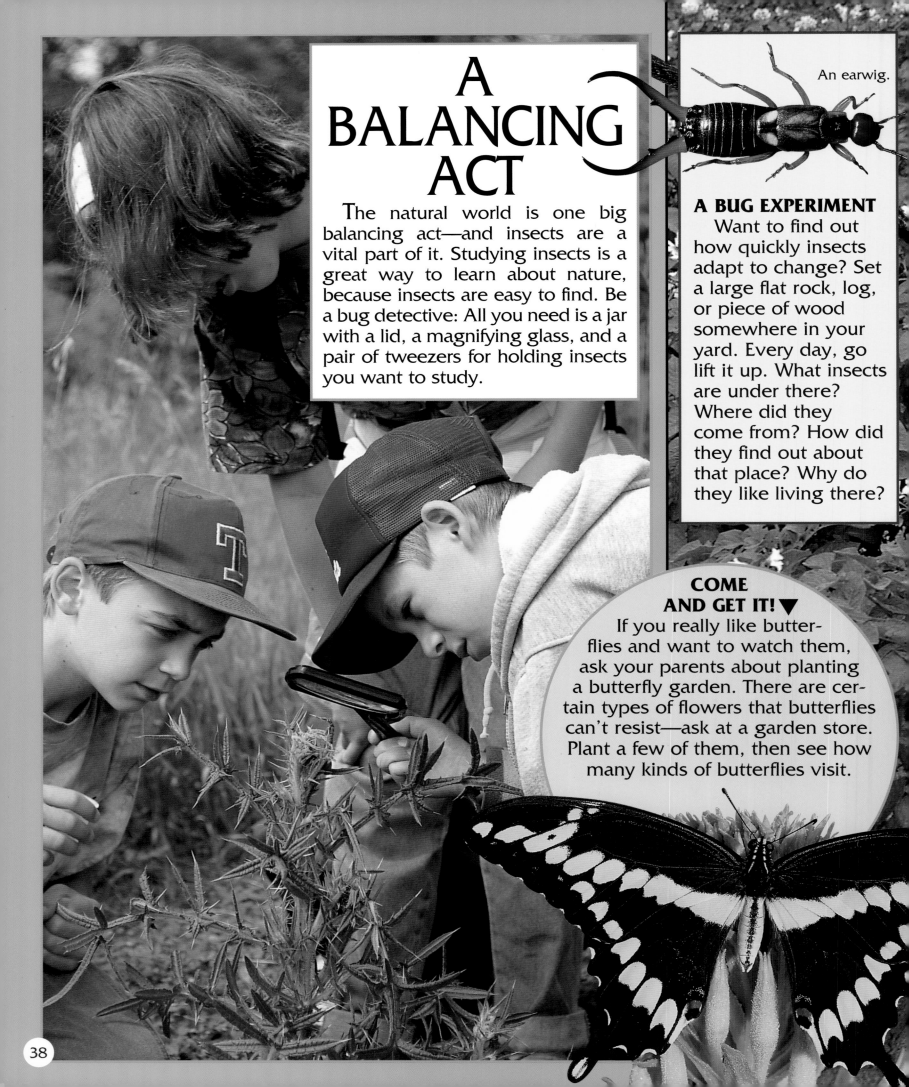

A BALANCING ACT

The natural world is one big balancing act—and insects are a vital part of it. Studying insects is a great way to learn about nature, because insects are easy to find. Be a bug detective: All you need is a jar with a lid, a magnifying glass, and a pair of tweezers for holding insects you want to study.

An earwig.

A BUG EXPERIMENT
Want to find out how quickly insects adapt to change? Set a large flat rock, log, or piece of wood somewhere in your yard. Every day, go lift it up. What insects are under there? Where did they come from? How did they find out about that place? Why do they like living there?

COME AND GET IT! ▼
If you really like butterflies and want to watch them, ask your parents about planting a butterfly garden. There are certain types of flowers that butterflies can't resist—ask at a garden store. Plant a few of them, then see how many kinds of butterflies visit.

OUR CHANGING WORLD ▲

Many insects have adapted to one kind of *habitat* (natural home). People need homes, too, so every year a little more of the world's rain forests are cleared away. Birds, insects, and other rain-forest animals become extinct—and we lose some of what helps to preserve a delicate balance.

LEARNING MORE ▲

Almost everyone knows what a cockroach looks like, but what about a tiger beetle (above) or a camel cricket? If you want to learn more about insects, buy a field identification guide. You'll see pictures of insects that live in your area, along with notes on where they live and what they eat.

OUT OF BALANCE

Why is it so hard to keep insects from damaging crops? Because a field of crops isn't like a forest or meadow, where many different plants and animals live. A crop field has just one kind of plant and few animals. If a bad bug moves in, there are often no predators to eat it—and no other kinds of plants for that bug to eat. Crop fields don't have balance.

KEEPING THE BALANCE

Why care about insects—yellow jackets like these, for instance? Without these wasps to eat caterpillars, we might not have some of our favorite flowers, because the caterpillars would destroy them. We need many different kinds of plants and animals to keep nature in balance.

WEIRD AND WONDERFUL

There are some strange mammals out there. Australia's platypus and echidna are the only two members of a group known as monotremes—egg-laying mammals! Once their babies hatch, they are fed on their mother's milk just like other young mammals.

▲ Echidnas have only one natural enemy—humans!

▲ The platypus is an excellent swimmer. It uses its bill to stir up the river bottom for its meals— worms, shellfish, and insects.

NOT A CARTOON ▼

The real Tasmanian devil is a carnivorous marsupial, or pouched mammal, weighing up to 17 pounds. It lives on Tasmania, an island near Australia. Its strong teeth and jaws are very good for tearing and eating dead animals.

▲ OVERHEAD HOPPERS

The tree kangaroo is good at leaping from one tree to another, but it is rather clumsy on the ground. Compared to its ground-dwelling relatives, it has short back legs, but its long tail helps it stay balanced in the branches.

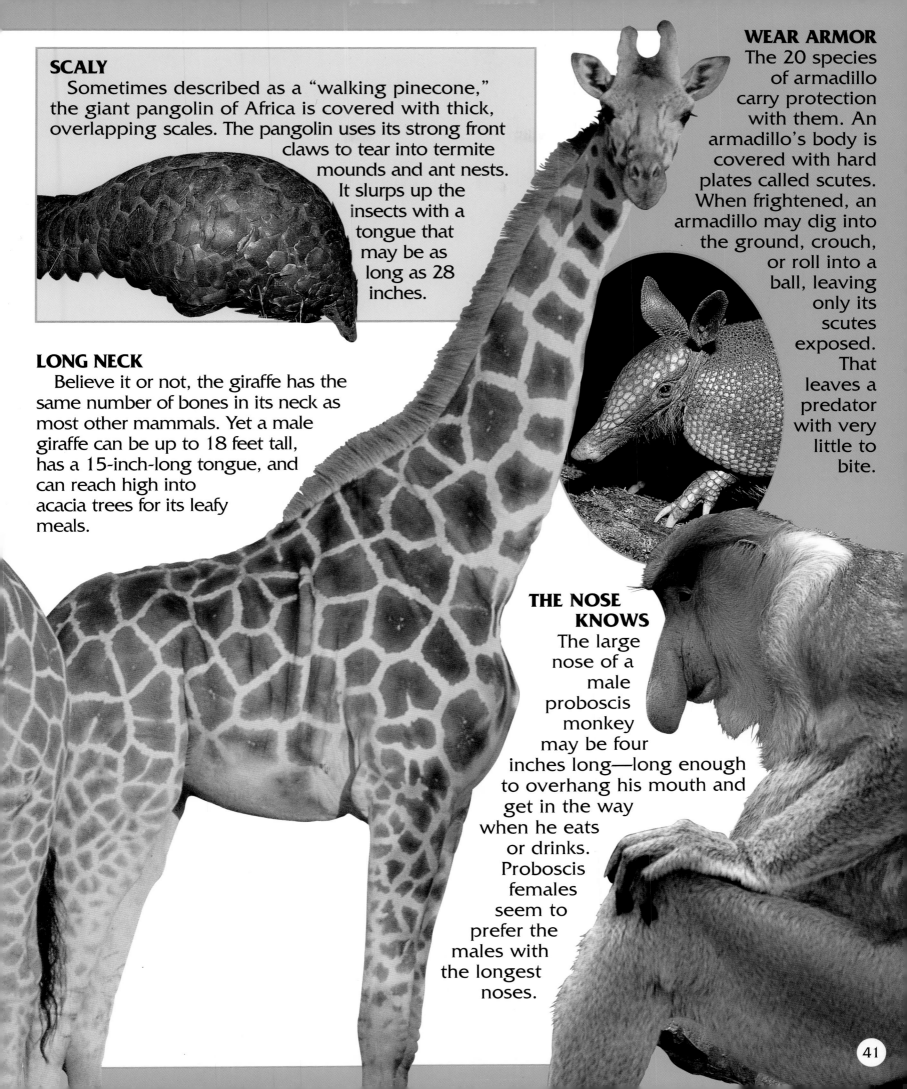

SCALY

Sometimes described as a "walking pinecone," the giant pangolin of Africa is covered with thick, overlapping scales. The pangolin uses its strong front claws to tear into termite mounds and ant nests. It slurps up the insects with a tongue that may be as long as 28 inches.

LONG NECK

Believe it or not, the giraffe has the same number of bones in its neck as most other mammals. Yet a male giraffe can be up to 18 feet tall, has a 15-inch-long tongue, and can reach high into acacia trees for its leafy meals.

WEAR ARMOR

The 20 species of armadillo carry protection with them. An armadillo's body is covered with hard plates called scutes. When frightened, an armadillo may dig into the ground, crouch, or roll into a ball, leaving only its scutes exposed. That leaves a predator with very little to bite.

THE NOSE KNOWS

The large nose of a male proboscis monkey may be four inches long—long enough to overhang his mouth and get in the way when he eats or drinks. Proboscis females seem to prefer the males with the longest noses.

NATURAL ODDITIES

Imagine finding a new life form, or talking to animals. In nature, scientists encounter some pretty strange things, and engineer some weird ways of getting inside an animal's world.

▲DOWN DEEP

In the murky waters of the Amazon River, where light penetrates to only a few inches below the surface, many new species of fish are being discovered. Mostly blind, they rely on electrical signals to navigate the dark river water.

WHITE WONDER▼

Coloration exists for a reason in nature, often as camouflage against predators. That's why it's strange to find an animal with a color different from the norm—like this pure white emperor penguin spotted in Antarctica. Sometimes white animals are albinos, which lack pigment and have red eyes. However, this penguin is not an albino, but a kind of genetic mutant rarely seen.

◄ SPYING CRABS

How do you know if an animal is using its eyes, and not its sense of smell? Some scientists mounted a tiny spy camera above the eyes of a male horseshoe crab to make a film of what the crab saw—female crabs. Meanwhile, they monitored electrical responses in the nerves that connect the eyes to the brain. Back in the lab, male crabs who saw the film responded in much the same way as the crab on the loose, proving that the eyes were at work.

▼ZONKEY!

What happens when you cross a zebra with a donkey? You get a crossbreed, an offspring with a mix of genes from both parents. Through biotechnology, scientists may isolate a specific gene from one species and give it to another, creating new varieties of plants and animals.

SEEING DOUBLE ▲

In 1996, Dolly, a sheep in Scotland, became the first mammal ever cloned from adult cells. A clone is a genetic duplicate—an animal or plant that is identical to another. Scientists replace the DNA of an egg cell with the DNA from another cell. The egg then develops into a clone of the animal that provided the new genetic material.

◄ GROSS WORKS

Some ancient remedies are still used today. After reattaching fingers or toes, doctors may apply leeches—blood-sucking worms— to help keep tiny blood vessels from clogging. Maggots are used to remove dead flesh. And physicians sometimes pack deep wounds with the same thing used by Egyptians 4,000 years ago—sugar.

WEIRD EYES

MOLE TOUCH ▲

Moles spend most of their life tunneling through the ground, searching for food. They don't see very well. Sometimes their eyes are even covered over with skin. Moles can tell light from dark. But they rely much more on touch and smell to find prey and get around.

◀ CROSS EYES

The chameleon (kuh–MEAL–ee–un) can move each eye separately. It can look forward with one eye and backward with the other at the same time. So how can a fly stay very close to this lizard without being seen, and eaten? The fly just sits on the chameleon's head exactly between its eyes!

44

▼ BIG EYES

Horseflies depend on their eyes to help them find food, avoid predators, and move around. They have eyes with lots of tiny lenses. Humans have a single lens.

SNAP SHOT ▲

A scallop may have as many as 100 tiny eyes. They are scattered in the fringe of tentacles around the shell. Each eye is only about the thickness of a dime! Scallop eyes don't form clear pictures, but they are very good at seeing movement. When a scallop sees a predator coming toward it, the scallop snaps its shell shut!

▼ PROTECTIVE EYES

The eyes of the conch (KAHNK) are at the end of movable stalks. The conch is like a big snail. It can pull its eyes back into the protection of its big, heavy shell.

▼ BULGING EYEBALLS

Mudskippers are strange fish. They spend hours out of the water sitting on the roots of mangrove trees! Their bulging, movable eyes work well underwater. Out of water, they can only see things that are very close.

FAKE EYES ▼

The eyespots on the rear end of this caterpillar certainly might confuse an attacking bird. The spots also draw attention away from the caterpillar's head.

45

VULTURE CULTURE

As gruesome as they may seem, vultures play a very important role: They clean up. Without vultures, rotting carcasses would spread disease, not to mention stink up things! It is believed that vultures in Africa eat more meat than do all the other predators combined.

LET'S MEAT UP

Up to six kinds of vultures may gather at a large carcass in Africa. Large vultures, like the lappet-faced vulture (left), may be the only ones capable of ripping into the fresh carcass of a large animal, or eating tough parts such as bone and skin. Smaller vultures follow, eating the softer parts, sometimes climbing right inside a carcass to get at the meat.

◀ BALD IS BEAUTIFUL

It makes perfect sense that the king vulture has a bare head, because this carrion-eating bird sticks its head into gooey, rotting carcasses. After eating, most vultures enjoy a bath and will sometimes fly a great distance to find water.

LIKE A STORK?

Unlike their Old World relatives, vultures in the Americas, such as these black vultures, are more closely related to storks than to birds of prey. They have a keen sense of smell, while Old World vultures rely on sight and can locate food only in open country.

BONE DROP▼

Bearded vultures, or lammergeiers, prefer to eat bones. Small bones are swallowed whole, but bigger ones pose a problem. So bearded vultures carry the bones into the sky, as high up as 200 feet, then drop them onto the rocks below, breaking them into edible bits. The vultures employ the same strategy with tortoises.

EGGS-ACTLY ▶

Egyptian vultures like to eat ostrich eggs, and they crack them open in a very interesting way. Small eggs are just picked up and thrown down. When eggs are too big to pick up, the vultures pick up stones and throw them until the eggs break—one of the few examples of tool use by an animal.

▼SMELL THAT?

The turkey vulture has an exceptionally good sense of smell, and can find carrion hidden beneath the rainforest canopy. It can tell the difference between edible meat and stuff that has become too rotten even for a vulture.

DAD DOES IT

Some animal fathers play a big part in raising their young. This male midwife toad is carrying his future babies wrapped around his hind legs. He keeps the eggs damp so they don't dry out. When the tadpoles hatch, he will drop them into water.

◄ PIGGY BACK RIDE

A giant water bug, the female toebiter glues her eggs onto the male's back. He carries them around until they hatch into tiny toebiters.

◄ SINGLE DAD

This male jacana (juh-KAH-nuh) looks like he has feet growing out of his wings. Actually, he has a baby under there, tucked away for safety. A father jacana builds a nest, sits on the eggs, and then raises the chicks on his own.

IN A POUCH ▶

Female seahorses lay their eggs into a pouch on the male's stomach. The father carries the eggs around until, one by one, the tiny seahorses pop out.

MOUTH NEST ▼

The male sea catfish picks up the eggs shortly after the female lays them. He carries the eggs in his jaws. Since the male catfish can't eat with the eggs in his mouth, he lives off body fat until they hatch. Once the eggs hatch, he waits another two or three weeks until his young are self-sufficient.

▲PROTECTED BUBBLES

The male Siamese fighting fish builds a nest by blowing bubbles. He guards the eggs and the baby fish that hatch from them. If the babies leave the bubble nest, their father sucks them up and spits them back in to safety.

MICRO WEIRD

With powerful instruments, you can enter the world of the very small. An optical microscope gets you into the main parts of a cell, magnifying things up to 1,500 times. An electron microscope makes things more than 500,000 times life size. A scanning tunneling microscope, a type of electron microscope, can magnify up to one million times—bringing the structure of an atom into focus!

▼ BLOOD SUCKERS

The animal below is a tick, a creature related to spiders. All those legs help this parasite hang on to its host as it sucks its blood. Ticks mostly feed on deer and wild mice, but sometimes on humans. A tick's bite can transfer Lyme disease from infected animals to humans.

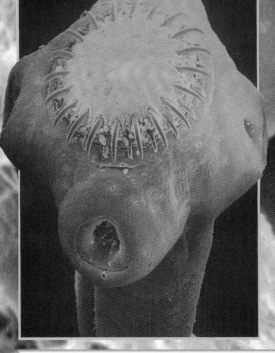

◀ In this photograph, blood cells are shown moving through the smallest branch of an artery.

INSIDE THE GUT ▲

Not all parasites live outside the host animal's body. Some, like this tapeworm, live inside it! Tapeworms live inside the gut of an animal—including humans. That crown of hooks on its head is how it holds on to its host.

The smallest tapeworms are only about 0.04 inch long. A few, however, can grow much bigger than microscope size—about 50 feet long. (A tapeworm like that would need a pretty big host!)

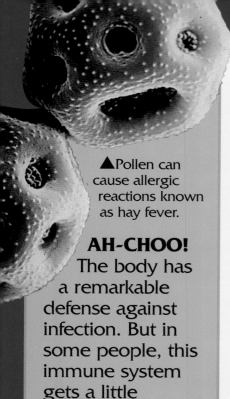

▲Pollen can cause allergic reactions known as hay fever.

AH-CHOO!

The body has a remarkable defense against infection. But in some people, this immune system gets a little confused. It recognizes certain harmless particles as dangerous and tries to fight them off. An allergic reaction is the result, which can be minor, like a sneeze, or, in extreme cases, life-threatening.

MICRO WARFARE

Viruses represent one of the biggest challenges to overcoming infectious diseases. When a virus, such as the common cold, invades a cell, it forces the cell to make copies of the virus. To attack the virus is to attack the body's own living cells. No cures exist, only preventive vaccines.

▲This weird-looking virus is responsible for causing warts.

TOUGH GUYS

You think you're tough? Some bacteria live in boiling hot water. Others survive radiation that would kill a human. Scientists have even found bacteria living 4,500 feet below the ground. These bacteria appear to survive in total darkness on nutrients they extract from the rocks.

MITE-Y SMALL

You never see them, but the tiny spider-relatives known as mites (left) are all around us, even in the cleanest house. They crawl through carpet, prowl your bed, and even live in your hair! But don't confuse them with the blood-sucking, foul-smelling insects known as bedbugs (above).

Mites actually help keep your house clean by feeding on flakes of dead skin.

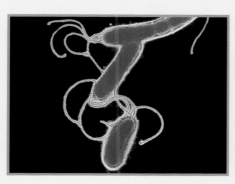

◀ BEACH BABIES

It's just a beach, or is it? Living in the sand is one of the richest animal communities found on Earth. These tiny meiofauna (MY-oh-faw-nah) are strange creatures—some have heads covered with whirling hairs, others cling to sand grains with hooked claws.

A single handful of wet sand may hold 10,000 of these animals.

LOADS OF LIZARDS

SUNBATHERS
Have you ever seen a lizard or any other reptile lying in the sun? These creatures are cold-blooded, and need the sun for warmth. In fact, if a lizard becomes too hot or too cold, its body doesn't work properly.

◀ The marine iguana

Meet the lizards. Some of these four-legged, scaly creatures can lap up an insect and then disappear before you can even blink. Like snakes, turtles, and crocodiles, lizards are reptiles—distant relatives of the dinosaurs.

The sungazer has spiny armor, which it uses for defense.

TOUGH GUY
A lizard's scaly skin is made of keratin, the same material found in your skin, nails, and hair. These tough scales protect the lizard's body from injury.

This Nile monitor lizard has netted a fish.

NO-FAIL TAIL
Most lizards spend their time on land, but some are strong swimmers. Their long, powerful tail helps propel them through the water.

LIZARD? NOT! ▶

Salamanders are often mistaken for lizards. They belong to a group of animals called amphibians, which include frogs, toads, and newts. Amphibian skin is soft and moist and without scales. Unlike reptiles, amphibians must lay their eggs in the water.

LIZARD OR SNAKE? ▲

Because its long, legless body resembles that of a snake, the glass lizard is often confused for one. But check its eyes. Like most other lizards, the glass lizard's eyes open and close. Snakes have no eyelids. Their eyes remain open all the time!

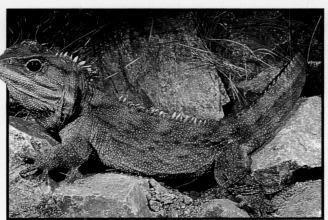

◀ ONE OF A KIND

Although lizardlike in appearance, the tuatara is not a lizard. It's the sole survivor of an ancient group of reptiles. Tuataras live on a few scattered islands near New Zealand. They make their home in burrows, which they leave at night to hunt insects.

LIVING ALL OVER

You can find lizards just about anywhere in the world except in cold regions. Many can be found in the tropics. They live in just about every kind of habitat, making their home in trees, water, and underground.

The Komodo dragon

The dwarf gecko

DWARFS TO DRAGONS ▲

Lizards range in size from the one-inch-long dwarf gecko to the ten-foot-long, 365-pound Komodo dragon—and even longer. Some of the smaller lizards fit in your hand, and they're not dangerous to hold. But a Komodo dragon will attack and even kill people!

LOTS OF LIZARDS

With more than 3,700 different species, lizards are by far the largest group of reptiles. You may have a picture in your mind of what a lizard is supposed to look like. But lizards look very different from one another. Just compare iguanas, monitors, chameleons, agamids, geckos, skinks, and some other, common lizards.

◀ SUPER GRIP

Most all lizards have five, clawed toes, and can scuttle up some kind of surface. Geckos probably have the most incredible grip, because they have brushlike hooks on their feet. They are often seen at night in houses in tropical regions, running across the ceilings or climbing the glass in windows! But geckos do even more. The most vocal lizards, they make a noise that sounds like..."geck-oh, geck-oh."

ALL-AMERICAN ▶

This lizard, known as an anole, is found only in the southern United States. It's known as the American "chameleon"

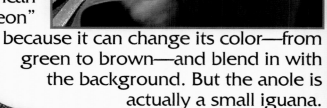

because it can change its color—from green to brown—and blend in with the background. But the anole is actually a small iguana.

MIGHTY MONITOR ▲

Among lizards, the monitors are the mightiest. There are about 30 different kinds, including the fierce Komodo dragon. Not all are huge, but the big ones are really big. The Nile monitor, which is medium-sized, grows up to seven feet.

◀ Two tokay geckos.

The green tree skink

TAIL OF THE SKINK

Found on every continent except Antarctica, skinks make up a family of over 1,000 different kinds. These lizards are fairly small but have very long tails—usually as long as their body!

The green iguana

IT'S AN IGUANA!

Ranging from southern Canada to almost the tip of South America, iguanas make up the largest lizard family, with over 700 different kinds. They live in many different habitats, such as deserts and rain forests, where they feed on plants. These hefty lizards can grow up to six feet long. Some have bizarre features, such as a large flap of skin around their neck, called a *dewlap*.

Male swifts may have patches of brilliant blue and green.

Male agamids are often brightly colored.

IN LIVING COLOR

You may think of lizards as being merely brown or green, but they actually get quite colorful. They can be spotted, speckled, or multicolored. Some, the chameleons especially, change color, from green to blue or even orange.

55

BODY HEAT

The web-footed gecko basks in the early morning sun. Only when its body has soaked up enough heat will it start hunting.

All reptiles are unable to produce their own body heat the way mammals and birds can. They need the sun's heat to warm their body. Because of their dependence on the sun, most lizards are found in places with warm climates. Many make their home in the desert.

Usually known for their bright colors, chameleons are a different story in the desert. Here, camouflage means blending in with sand and rock.

In the desert, the collared lizard hops from rock top to rock top in search of insects and smaller lizards to feed on.

NO SWEAT

Lizards don't sweat, or lose water through their thick, scaly skin. This ability allows them to live in dry desert climates. But there's a limit to how much heat they can stand. Desert temperatures sometimes reach 120°F. If a desert iguana's temperature rises above 110°F, it could die. To escape this danger, it has to find shade.

A desert iguana

This sand-diving lizard is checking the temperature.

DESERT DIG ▲

To escape the scorching midday sun, some lizards burrow below the surface of the sun-baked sand where the temperatures are cooler.

DANCING FEET ▲

When the sand becomes too hot to walk on, a shovel-snouted lizard begins a strange dance to find relief. First it lifts its two left feet off the burning sand, then its two right feet. For the final step, it lifts all four feet while it rests on its belly.

▼BURROWING GIANTS

Found only on a few small Indonesian islands, the Komodo dragon uses its ten, long, sharp claws to hollow out a burrow in the side of a small hill. Here is where it escapes the hot midday sun, and where it snuggles for warmth when the sun goes down.

WHAT'S FOR DINNER?

Most lizards are meat eaters, dining on insects and other prey. Their small, sharp teeth grab and hold their catch while their jaws make a series of quick, snapping movements over the animal. Then they swallow the prey whole.

Having ▶ snared a rodent, this tegu is swallowing its prey.

▲ GREAT SHOT

In less than one second, the chameleon can catch dinner. Its tongue is an amazing hunting weapon. Stretching the combined length of the chameleon's body and tail, the tongue has at its end a sticky pad that picks up insects. Once dinner is attached, the tongue will recoil back inside the mouth.

CACTUS EATERS

Some lizards, such as iguanas and agamids, are vegetarians, preferring to eat plants rather than animals for dinner. It may seem astounding, but iguanas can bite into and eat cactus without so much as an "ouch."

NIGHT HUNTERS

All geckos are meat eaters, and most are active at night. They feed mainly on insects and spiders, but the larger geckos can overpower other lizards, birds, and even small mammals. The geckos that make good night hunters have huge eyes like a cat's. The vertical pupils open wide at night to let in as much light as possible.

EGG EATERS ▶

The venomous Gila (HE-luh) monster is one of only two poisonous lizards in the world. Found in the south-western United States, the Gila monster crawls too slowly to chase down its dinner. Instead, it feeds on eggs and newborn animals.

HEARTY APPETITE

The Komodo dragon is so big that it eats goats, pigs, and deer. With sharp teeth like a shark's, a dragon can finish off a sixty-pound dinner in about fifteen minutes.

▼ TASTING AIR

Some lizards, like the monitors, taste the air with a forked tongue, much like snakes do. In this way, lizards can track down prey and avoid predators.

GETTING AROUND

Lizards depend on quickness to hunt and keep safe. Most have four legs and use them to move at high speeds. Nature has also given these creatures extra equipment, custom-designed for the places in which they live.

DEEP-SEA DIVER

The marine iguana of the Galapagos Islands is the only lizard truly at home in saltwater. A vegetarian with little to choose from on the island, the iguana dives as deep as thirty feet to find seaweed and algae. While diving for food, the marine iguana can stop its heart completely for three minutes in order to save oxygen.

FLYING DRAGON ▶

When the agamid known as the flying dragon spots a green vine snake slithering closer and closer, it moves into action. It raises up and expands the loose flaps of skin along its body in an attempt to look larger and more ferocious. Right before the snake strikes, this tricky lizard glides safely to a nearby tree.

WORMY LIZARD ▼

Not all lizards have four legs, especially not the ones that live underground. Some have only two legs or no legs at all. Without legs, it's easier to slither through the earth, tunneling in search of insects and worms.

This two-legged worm lizard lives in the Sonoran Desert in Baja, Mexico.

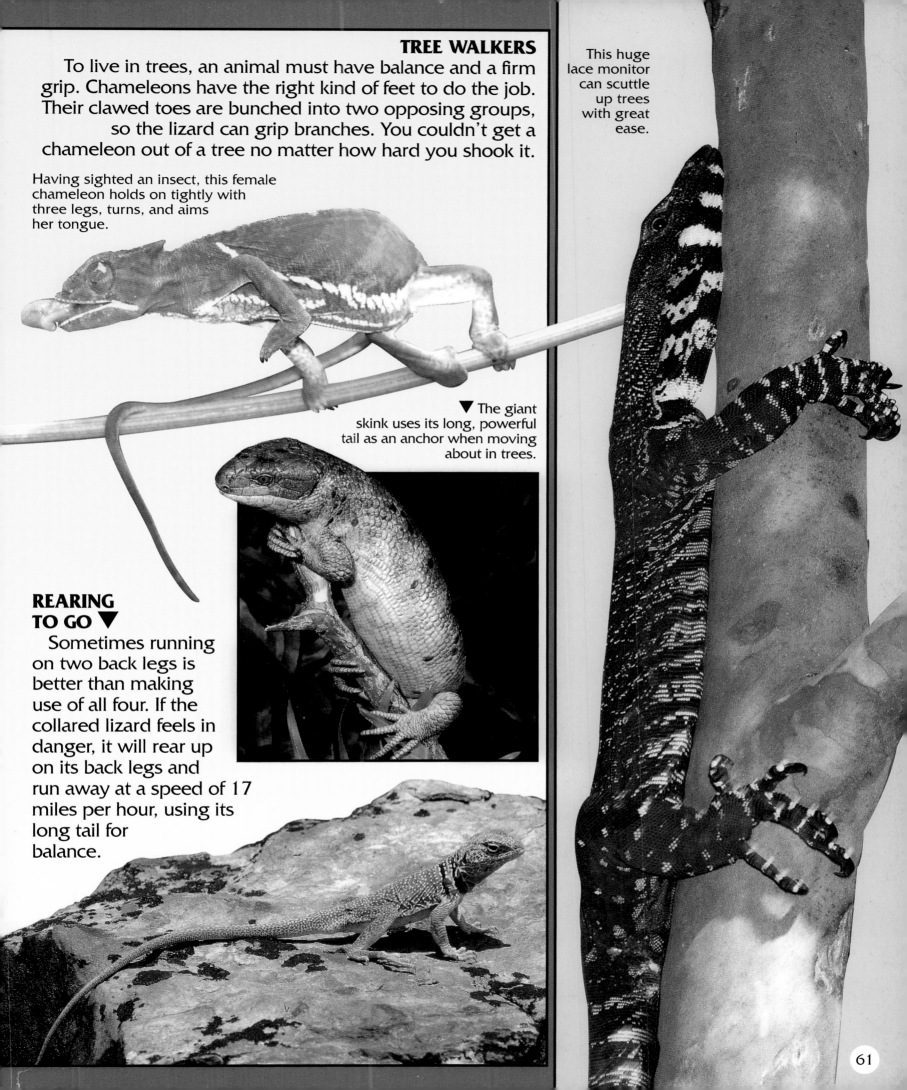

TREE WALKERS

To live in trees, an animal must have balance and a firm grip. Chameleons have the right kind of feet to do the job. Their clawed toes are bunched into two opposing groups, so the lizard can grip branches. You couldn't get a chameleon out of a tree no matter how hard you shook it.

Having sighted an insect, this female chameleon holds on tightly with three legs, turns, and aims her tongue.

This huge lace monitor can scuttle up trees with great ease.

▼ The giant skink uses its long, powerful tail as an anchor when moving about in trees.

REARING TO GO ▼

Sometimes running on two back legs is better than making use of all four. If the collared lizard feels in danger, it will rear up on its back legs and run away at a speed of 17 miles per hour, using its long tail for balance.

KINGS OF COLOR

If you want to see spectacular lizards, look at chameleons. There are about 85 different kinds, and they all have amazing equipment. They have a tongue as long as their body, eyes that can look in two different directions at one time, and a specialized tail and clawed feet that keep them secure in the branches. But chameleons are probably best known for their amazing color changes.

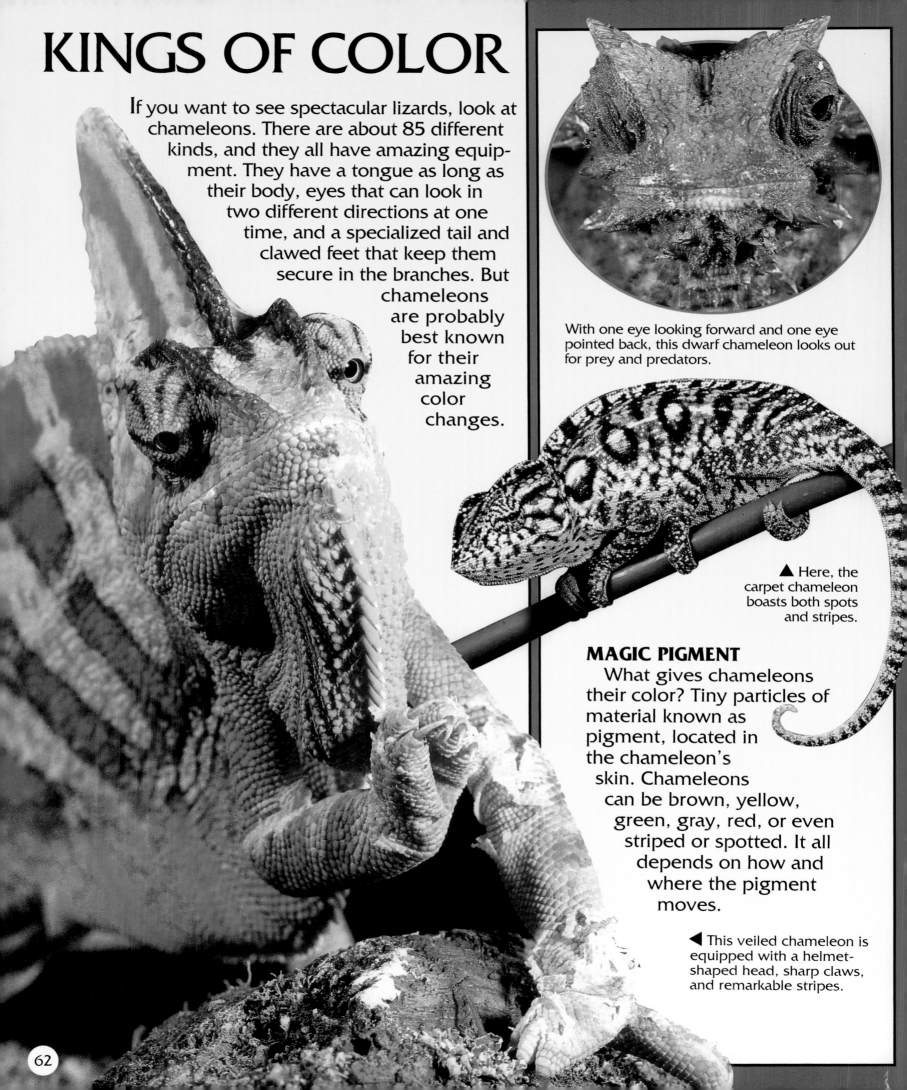

With one eye looking forward and one eye pointed back, this dwarf chameleon looks out for prey and predators.

▲ Here, the carpet chameleon boasts both spots and stripes.

MAGIC PIGMENT

What gives chameleons their color? Tiny particles of material known as pigment, located in the chameleon's skin. Chameleons can be brown, yellow, green, gray, red, or even striped or spotted. It all depends on how and where the pigment moves.

◀ This veiled chameleon is equipped with a helmet-shaped head, sharp claws, and remarkable stripes.

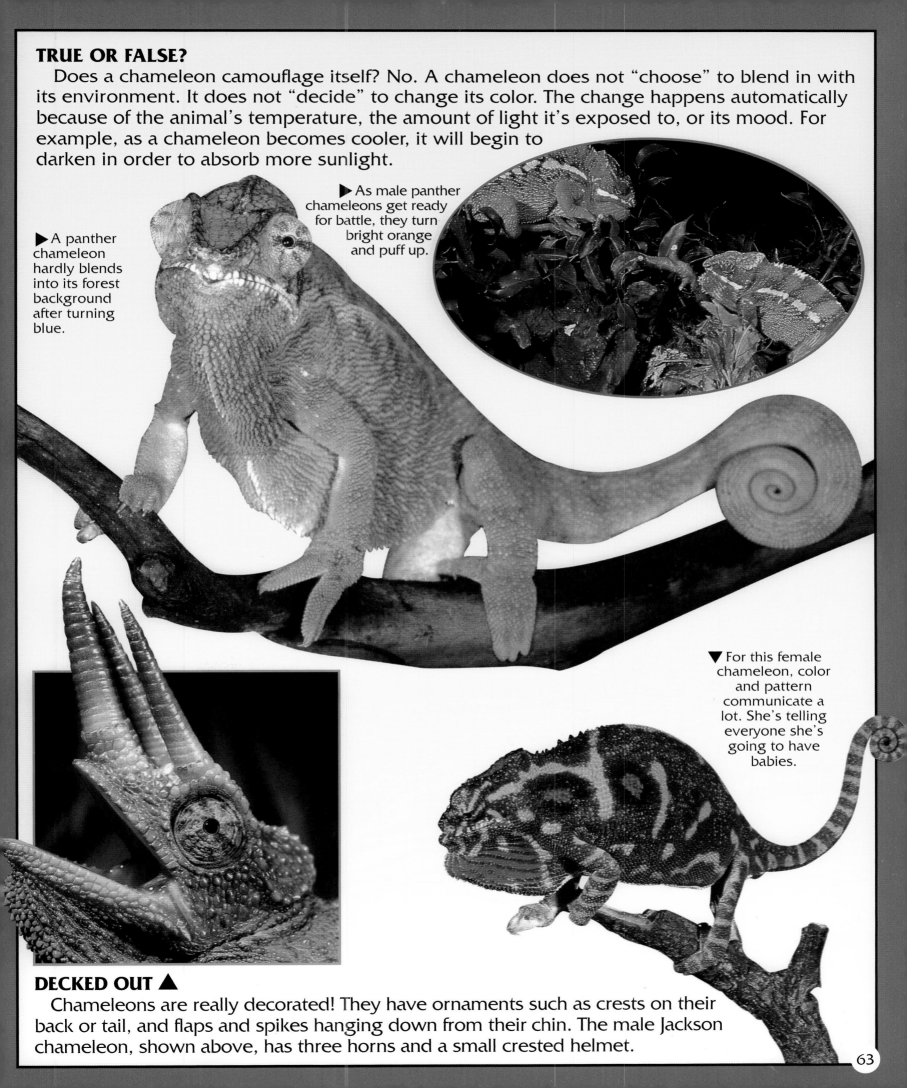

TRUE OR FALSE?

Does a chameleon camouflage itself? No. A chameleon does not "choose" to blend in with its environment. It does not "decide" to change its color. The change happens automatically because of the animal's temperature, the amount of light it's exposed to, or its mood. For example, as a chameleon becomes cooler, it will begin to darken in order to absorb more sunlight.

► A panther chameleon hardly blends into its forest background after turning blue.

► As male panther chameleons get ready for battle, they turn bright orange and puff up.

▼ For this female chameleon, color and pattern communicate a lot. She's telling everyone she's going to have babies.

DECKED OUT ▲

Chameleons are really decorated! They have ornaments such as crests on their back or tail, and flaps and spikes hanging down from their chin. The male Jackson chameleon, shown above, has three horns and a small crested helmet.

63

BABY BOOM

From courtship to birth, baby-making varies from one kind of lizard to another. Usually when courting, males become more brightly colored. But some also do special "dances" to get a female's attention. Most females lay eggs and leave their unhatched babies behind. But some carry the eggs inside their body until they're ready to hatch.

LITTLE IGUANAS

Most mother lizards lay eggs with tough, leathery shells. The green iguana may lay up to 40 at one time. The baby lizards that emerge from the eggs are miniature versions of their parents. Right after they hatch, the babies can find their own food.

WRESTLE MANIA

At the start of each mating season, male Bengal monitor lizards try to impress the ladies with their strength. They wrestle each other for the privilege of mating with a female. It may look like a dance, but it's serious business!

When the ▶ male African rainbow agama wants to get a female's attention, he completes a series of push-ups.

CHISELING OUT

All baby lizards that hatch from eggs have a pointed *egg tooth* on their snout. They use the tooth to chisel their way out of the eggshell.

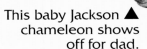

▲ THANKS, MOM

The five-lined skink mother doesn't leave her babies to fend for themselves. She coils herself around her eggs and guards them against egg-eating predators.

▲ Collared lizards hatch from laid eggs.

BIRTHDAY

In cooler climates, eggs buried in the ground would not stay warm enough to hatch. In these places, lizards incubate the eggs inside their body, where it is warm. Some lizards, such as the Jackson chameleon, give birth to fully developed babies.

This baby Jackson ▲ chameleon shows off for dad.

▼ Bearded dragon babies

SAFETY IN NUMBERS

Lizard babies may start fighting each other very early on, trying to establish a territory. But some babies stick together until they're old enough to take care of themselves. For the first twelve months of life, emerald lizards stay together. When attacked, they scatter in all directions, confusing their attacker and giving themselves a few seconds to escape.

THAT'S AMAZING!

Have you ever seen a lizard with a beard? Do you know there's one lizard that can walk on water? Lizards are amazing. Their antics and armor really set them apart!

◀ WALKING ON WATER

The basilisk lizard has an incredible method of escape from its enemies. It rears up on its hind legs and runs across the surface of water. Moving quickly on long, wide toes, the basilisk can take several strides before its body breaks the water's surface and sinks in.

BIG BEARD ▶

This lizard does have a beard—a chin full of spiky armor! Known as the bearded dragon, it uses its armor to frighten enemies. It inflates its body, opens its mouth, and expands its big, spiny throat. That's a frightening sight and a big signal to stand clear!

SALT SHAKERS

Marine iguanas are really resourceful when it comes to finding food. They swim the sea looking for seaweed. There's one problem, though. They swallow a large amount of water and get a huge overdose of salt. But their body has developed an amazing trick. It shakes out the salt through special glands in the nasal cavities.

NO-FAIL TAIL

The chameleon is one lizard that can hang by its tail from a branch like a monkey. All lizards have fantastic tails. Some tails are long and are used for balance. Some can be discarded to distract enemies so that the lizard can escape. But only a few are built for strength and allow the lizard to hang out in trees.

THIRST QUENCHER

Getting a drink of water in the desert is not that easy, unless you're a thorny devil. This lizard has sharp spikes covering its body for protection. But the spikes also provide drinking water. Overnight, dew condenses on the thorns, and the water trickles along tiny grooves in the skin to the thorny devil's mouth.

WINDSHIELD WIPER

Most lizards have eyelids, which protect the eyes and help keep them clean. Geckos, however, do not. Instead, they use their long tongue like a windshield wiper, rolling it over their eyes to keep their vision clear!

BYE-BYE SKIN

Lizards never stop growing! Because their skin does not grow with them, they have to shed it. A few use shedding as a defense. Geckos are covered with a very loose layer of skin. The slightest amount of pressure from an attack causes the skin to come off. The lizard escapes, and the attacker is left with an old suit.

RUN OR HIDE

Lizards are survivors. One of the reasons they are so successful is that they've developed very effective ways to defend themselves. Most lizards are small creatures who depend on speed and quickness rather than brute strength. Their first line of defense, in fact, is to run or hide.

TIGHT SQUEEZE ▼

While basking in the sun, lizards like to stay close to a rocky crevice or burrow where they can retreat if threatened. But the chuckwalla lizard has an additional defense. When it gets between two rocks, it takes several deep breaths and inflates its body with air. Wedged in tightly, the chuckwalla becomes impossible for an attacker to even budge.

IN THE HOLE ▼

Hiding can be very simple in the desert. A lizard can simply burrow beneath the sand. With only its face showing, this sandy-colored horned lizard could easily be overlooked by a predator.

GOOD PLANNING ▲

A basilisk lizard knows how to take a nap. Living in Brazil's tropical rain forest, it crawls out to the tip of a thin branch that extends out over a small stream. When a hungry snake slithers too close, the branch shakes. With this warning, the basilisk drops into the water, safely out of the snake's reach.

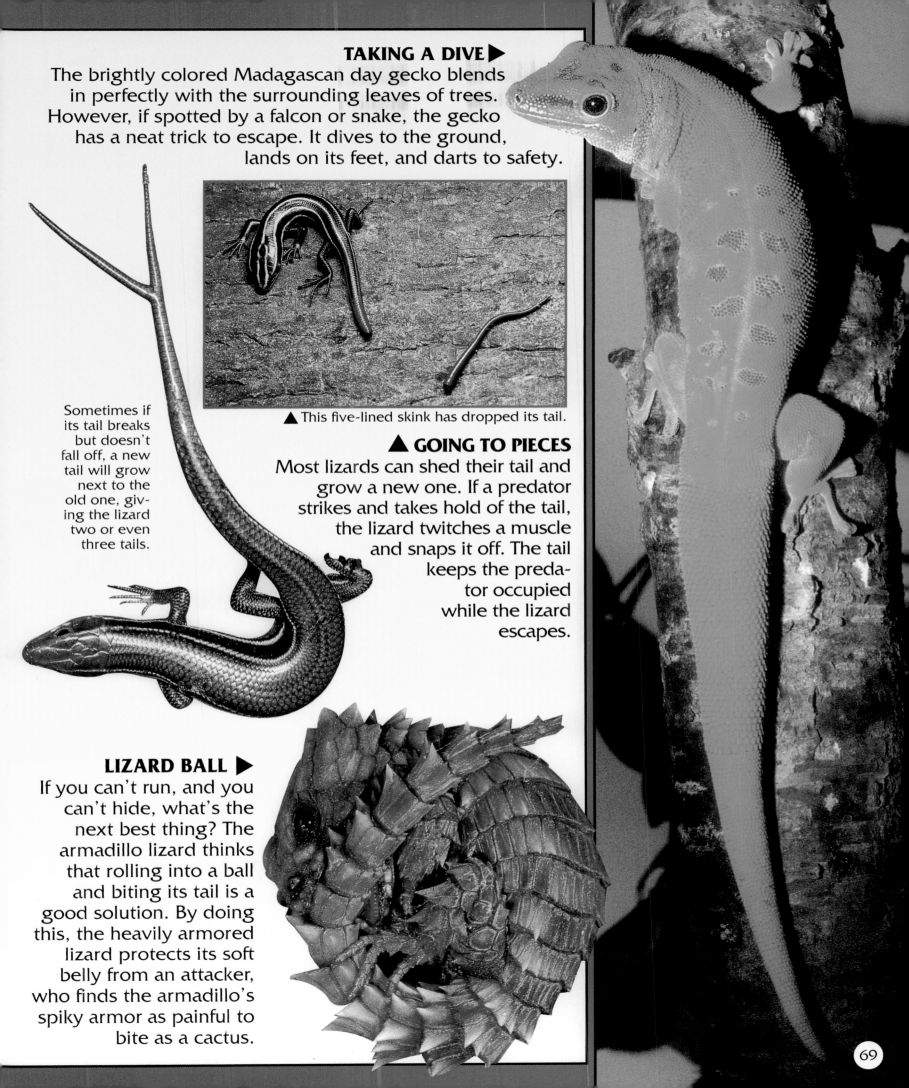

TAKING A DIVE ▶

The brightly colored Madagascan day gecko blends in perfectly with the surrounding leaves of trees. However, if spotted by a falcon or snake, the gecko has a neat trick to escape. It dives to the ground, lands on its feet, and darts to safety.

▲ This five-lined skink has dropped its tail.

Sometimes if its tail breaks but doesn't fall off, a new tail will grow next to the old one, giving the lizard two or even three tails.

▲ GOING TO PIECES

Most lizards can shed their tail and grow a new one. If a predator strikes and takes hold of the tail, the lizard twitches a muscle and snaps it off. The tail keeps the predator occupied while the lizard escapes.

LIZARD BALL ▶

If you can't run, and you can't hide, what's the next best thing? The armadillo lizard thinks that rolling into a ball and biting its tail is a good solution. By doing this, the heavily armored lizard protects its soft belly from an attacker, who finds the armadillo's spiky armor as painful to bite as a cactus.

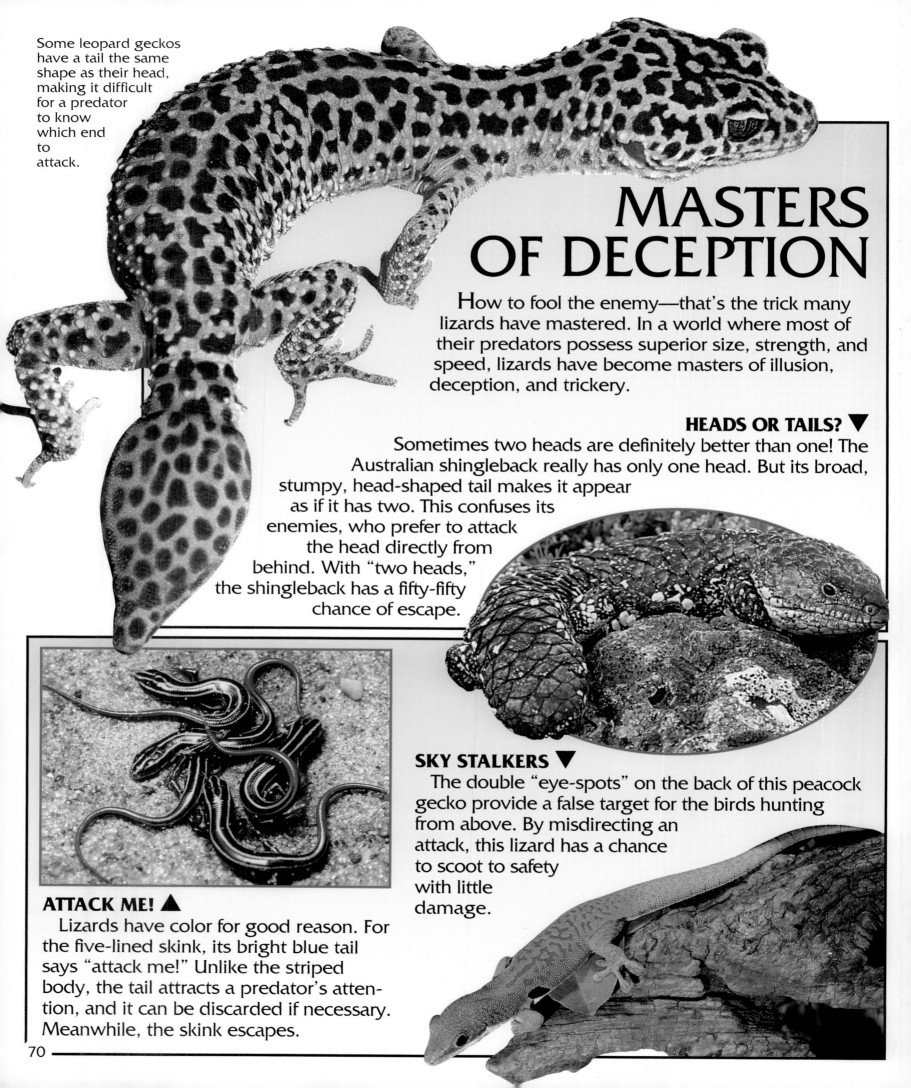

Some leopard geckos have a tail the same shape as their head, making it difficult for a predator to know which end to attack.

MASTERS OF DECEPTION

How to fool the enemy—that's the trick many lizards have mastered. In a world where most of their predators possess superior size, strength, and speed, lizards have become masters of illusion, deception, and trickery.

HEADS OR TAILS? ▼

Sometimes two heads are definitely better than one! The Australian shingleback really has only one head. But its broad, stumpy, head-shaped tail makes it appear as if it has two. This confuses its enemies, who prefer to attack the head directly from behind. With "two heads," the shingleback has a fifty-fifty chance of escape.

SKY STALKERS ▼

The double "eye-spots" on the back of this peacock gecko provide a false target for the birds hunting from above. By misdirecting an attack, this lizard has a chance to scoot to safety with little damage.

ATTACK ME! ▲

Lizards have color for good reason. For the five-lined skink, its bright blue tail says "attack me!" Unlike the striped body, the tail attracts a predator's attention, and it can be discarded if necessary. Meanwhile, the skink escapes.

WHERE'S THAT LIZARD?

Camouflage is a nifty little trick. Many lizards are naturally colored to blend in with their habitat, whether it's in the trees of a rain forest, in the desert sand, or on a forest floor.

▲ If you were walking by this tree, would you see this leaf-tailed gecko?

▲ Can you spot a gliding gecko in this photo?

A panther chameleon

FREEZE!

True masters of deception, chameleons know that, when you want to escape a predator, it's sometimes better just to stand still. In the face of danger, chameleons stop and remain motionless. Their color usually blends with their environment, making them doubly hard to spot. An attacker will often go right on by.

PLAYING POSSUM

Some chameleons "play possum," or pretend to be dead. When cornered, the chameleon suddenly drops to the ground on its side, stretches its feet out stiffly, and remains motionless. Most predators prefer a fresh kill to a dead meal, so they sometimes walk away. If not, they at least relax their guard long enough so that the chameleon can run to safety.

SCARY MOVES

When escape is blocked and a hungry predator is closing in, nature has provided lizards with one last line of defense. A lizard will turn aggressive, trying to scare or intimidate its would-be killer into backing down. If that fails, watch out! The lizard will attack.

▼ STAY AWAY!

If cornered, the Australian frilled lizard rears up on its hind legs, opens its mouth wide, and unfolds the enormous frill around its head. If its attacker is still around, the lizard swings its head to and fro, lashes its long, whiplike tail back and forth, and sounds a long, angry hissss!

POP EYES

A frightened helmeted lizard tries to make himself look as large and ferocious as possible. It raises the bony "helmet" on the back of its skull, inflates the flap of skin around its neck, and bugs out its eyes. After seeing this huge frightening head, many predators realize that they weren't quite as hungry as they thought.

◀ This anole tries to frighten off an intruder by inflating a brightly colored dewlap.

CRYING BLOOD

Horned toads are small lizards with toad-like faces. Their bodies are covered with razor-sharp "horns" or spikes. When cornered, the horny toad will shoot small jets of blood from its eyes. Some people think the blood irritates the eyes of an attacker, but perhaps it just frightens them.

SURPRISE!

◄When threatened, the Australian blue-tongued skink sticks out its bright blue tongue and waves it around. This sudden and unexpected flash of color can startle an attacker long enough for the skink to escape.

◄The Mexican beaded lizard is one of only two poisonous lizards.

SLOW DEATH

The Mexican beaded lizard and Gila (HE-luh) monster are poisonous. Once they bite their enemy, they clamp onto it with their teeth. As the lizard struggles to keep its grip, the poison slowly trickles into the wound. The lizard's venom can kill a small animal but rarely kills people.

A LOOK AHEAD

Today a great many lizards are in danger of being killed, due mainly to loss of habitat and hunting. People can help prevent their endangerment. By not purchasing products made from lizards, they can give hunters fewer reasons to kill these incredible creatures.

Dumeril's monitor

Pacific monitor

A TASTY TREAT ▼

Believe it or not, some people find lizards to be tasty treats. In South and Central America, iguanas are a delicacy often served to visiting relatives and important guests. However, this custom is not a huge threat to the lizard population.

THE PRICE OF BEAUTY ▲

Monitor lizards are beautiful, but they pay a price. Although it is illegal to hunt them, monitors are killed for their skin, which is used to make lizard-skin boots and shoes, pocketbooks, belts, wallets, and briefcases.

POPULAR PETS

For some people, having an exotic pet like a lizard is fashionable. But many lizards die while being captured or transported to pet shops. Of those that survive, a great many die because they are unhappy and unaccustomed to living in captivity.

◄ DEADLY COMPETITION

For years, the Galapagos Island iguana was hunted for sport. Today, something else threatens its existence. Goats, brought onto the island by farmers and ranchers, compete with the iguana for available but scarce plant life.

DRAGON SLAYERS ▼

Farmers shoot Komodo dragons to protect livestock, but they are not the only dragon slayers. To many people, the Komodo dragon is a frightening creature. Out of this fear and a lack of knowledge, many Komodos have been killed. There are fewer than 1,000 Komodo dragons left. Their endangerment has prompted the Indonesian government to make it illegal to kill them. Now these well known dragons are a treasured tourist attraction.

▲ HABITAT DESTRUCTION

Because the trees in which it lives are being razed, and the land is being cleared for homes, the long-tailed Fijian banded iguana is in serious trouble. Having lost much of its habitat, there is nowhere to hide newly laid eggs, which become easy pickings for the banded iguana's enemy, the mongoose.

Photo Credits

- iStock: Cover; End Pages (Front); pages 4-5, 6-7, 9, 10, 12-13, 48-49, 50
- Digital Vision/Litle Creatures: pages 2-3
- PhotoDisc/Sea Life: End Pages (Back)
- Jeff Rotman Photography: pages 4-5
- Fred Bavendam/Minden: pages 6-7, 10-12
- Norbert Wu: pages 14-15, 45, 49
- David Fleetham/Visuals Unlimited: pages 6-7, 8-9
- Minden Pictures: pages 6-7
- David Wrobel Visuals Unlimited: pages 10-12
- HPH Photography/The Wildlife Collection: pages 12-13
- Marty Codano/DRK: page 14
- Bill Beatty/Visuals Unlimited: pages 12-13, 29, 33, 36, 38
- Stephen Frink: pages 12-13
- Al Giddings Images Inc.: page 15
- Dr. Bruce Robison/Minden Pictures: page 14
- Marty Snyderman/Waterhouse Stock Photography: page 15
- Dwight Kuhn: pages 19-20, 22-23, 27, 29, 35, 38-39, 49, 53-54, 58-59, 67
- Tom & Pat Leeson: pages 24, 47
- Robert & Linda Mitchell: End Pages (Front); pages 16-18, 20-23, 26-35, 37, 39, 48
- A. B. Sheldon: pages 37, 45, 65, 69-70
- Lynn M. Stone: pages 26, 47
- Alabama Bureau of Tourism: page 36
- Stanley Breeden/DRK: pages 27-27, 61, 72
- Fred Bruemmer/DRK: pages 26-27
- D. Cavagnaro/DRK: page 32
- Marty Cordano/DRK: page 30
- Michael Fogden/DRK: pages 25, 56-57, 67, 72-73
- John Gerlach/DRK: page 38
- Stephen J. Krasemann/DRK: pages 19, 26, 31
- Sid and Shirley Rucker/DRK: page 25
- John Winnie Jr./DRK: page 19
- Robert Calentine/Visuals Unlimited: page 34
- L. J. Connor/Visuals Unlimited: page 37
- John D. Cunningham/Visuals Unlimited: page 16
- Carlyn B. Galati/Visuals Unlimited: page 33
- Barbara Gerlach/Visuals Unlimited: page 19
- Tim Hauf/Visuals Unlimited: page 39
- Ken Lucas/Visuals Unlimited: pages 18, 55, 74-75
- Steve McCutcheon/Visuals Unlimited: page 34
- Kjell B. Sandved/Visuals Unlimited: pages 25, 28, 44-45, 71
- Science VU/Visuals Unlimited: page 30
- Leroy Simon/Visuals Unlimited: page 16
- Milton H. Tierney Jr./Visuals Unlimited: page 22
- Richard Walters/Visuals Unlimited: pages 35, 44-45
- William J. Weber/Visuals Unlimited: page 23
- Rick & Nora Bowers/Wildlife Collection: page 24
- Ken Deitcher/Wildlife Collection: page 27
- Charles Melton/Wildlife Collection: page 32
- Kevin Schafer: pages 40-51
- Ford Kristo/DRK: page 40
- Gerry Ellis: ENP Images: page 40
- Peter Pickford/DRK: page 41
- Tom DiMauro/Wildlife Collection: page 41
- Martin Harvey/ Wildlife Collection: pages 40, 45-47, 52, 57, 62
- R. Barlow: page 42
- Gerald L. Kooyman: page 42
- John Lundberg & John Sullivan: page 42
- AP Photo/Michael Stephens: page 43
- James Holmes/Cellmark Diagnostics/Science Photo Library: page 43
- Shahn Kermani/Gamma Liaison: page 43
- Richard Herrmann/Wildlife Collection: page 45
- Mary Besth Angelo/Photo Researchers: page 44
- M. P. Kahl/DRK: page 47
- Gerard & Buff Corsi/Visuals Unlimited: page 46
- Gil Lopez-Espina/Visuals Unlimited: page 47
- David Scharf: pages 50-51
- Dr. Tony Brain/Science Photo Library: page 51
- A.B. Dowsett/Science Photo Library: page 51
- K.H. Kjeldsen/Science Photo Library: page 51
- G. Shih R. Kessel/ Visuals Unlimited: page 50
- David M. Phillips/Visuals Unlimited: pages 50-51
- Breck P. Kent: pages 53-54, 56, 65, 67-68
- Zig Leszczynski: pages 44, 52-53, 57-65, 68-72, 74
- Dan Nedrelo: page 69
- John Cancalosi/DRK: pages 70, 73
- M.C. Chamberlain/DRK: page 61
- Joe McDonald/DRK: page 73
- David Northcott/DRK: pages 55, 63
- T.A. Wiewandt/DRK: page 60
- Jeremy Woodhouse/DRK: page 54
- Belinda Wright/DRK: page 72
- Stephen Dalton/Photo Researchers: page 66
- Nathan W. Cohen/Visuals Unlimited: page 75
- Gerald & Buff Corsi/Visuals Unlimited: page 66
- John Gerlach/Visuals Unlimited: page 61
- Thomas Gula/Visuals Unlimited: page 53
- Joe McDonald/Visuals Unlimited: pages 52, 62, 64, 69, 71
- Jim Merli/Visuals Unlimited: pages 59, 65-67
- David L. Pearson/Visuals Unlimited: page 55
- Dennis Frieborn/Wildlife Collection: page 58
- Mauricio Handler/Wildlife Collection: page 60
- Tim Laman/Wildlife Collection: page 53
- Minden Pictures/Fred Bavendam: page 10
- Minden Pictures/Dr. Bruce Robison: page 14
- Visuals Unlimited/G. Shih-R. Kessel: page 50